Railway World

ANNUAL 1986

£4.95

Previous page:
In the early years of the Great Western Society, a notable achievement was the operation of a passenger service on the BR Wallingford branch on several occasions. '1400' 0-4-2T No 1466 propels an auto-trailer out of Cholsey on 21 September 1968.
Mike Esau

This page:
On the Peterborough–Leicester line Class 31 No 31.403 heads the 14.14 Norwich–Birmingham New Street near Ashwell on 21 April 1983. *John C. Baker*

Overleaf:
The Great Western Society's 'Modified Hall' No 6998 *Burton Agnes Hall* enjoyed its first outing after restoration on 1 October 1972, from Didcot to Tyseley and back. The special train approaches Tackley on the outward journey. *Chris Kapolka*

Railway World
ANNUAL 1986
Edited by David Percival

LONDON
IAN ALLAN LTD

First published 1985

ISBN 0 7110 1506 6

© Ian Allan Ltd 1985

Published by Ian Allan Ltd, Shepperton, Surrey;
and printed by Ian Allan Printing Ltd at their works
at Coombelands in Runnymede, England

Contents

Chamois Remembered

Charles Meacher

With the demise of steam in Scotland, some of the Region's 'B1' 4-6-0s were stored at Thornton Junction awaiting their call to the scrapyard. Nameplates and maker's plates were removed and deposited in the store so people would not be tempted to take unlawful possession of these collector's pieces. A former St Margarets engine, No 61029 *Chamois* was included in the forlorn line-up and, remembering my long association with this 'B1', I wanted to acquire a nameplate 'for old times sake'. When I applied to the stores controller in Glasgow for this memento I was invited to make an offer. This put me off the idea – maybe because I had not much to offer – but it would have made a nice souvenir, surmounted by a picture of the European antelope.

Left:
'. . . a big, dirty three-cylinder steam engine.' The author was probably thinking of a St Margarets 'V2' 2-6-2, but the description fits Dundee-based 'A2' Pacific No 60530 *Sayajirao*, standing at the depot on 15 April 1966. *W. Brian Alexander*

But I don't really need a nameplate to remind me of *Chamois*.

Spring was in the air that far-off day when I booked on duty at St Margarets at the unusual time – for my profession, anyway – of 9am. All that spoiled this unusually civilised shift was the prospect of having to oil a big, dirty three-cylinder steam engine.

After showing my face to the timekeeper I put my head through the open window of the running office and enquired what was on the 10.30am Portobello-Carlisle. 'Ah!' beamed the senior running foreman, Bob McKay, 'we've a guid yin for you this morning, Charlie – '1029. Brand new!' The prefix '6' was never verbally included and 'brand new' was a reference to the engine's appearance after a general overhaul.

The fact that Bob had a number to give me at that time of day, when the supply was drying up, was reason enough for this happy mood. Too often the engine sheet was a blank but, given a number, Bob cared not what this represented in reality; that was the concern of his subordinates, who included me as the driver. I smiled at his carefree style and, turning away from the window, saw my mate approaching with his ears cocked for the number. 'A "B1" this morning, George. '1029 – brand new!' The robust supervisor grinned even more as I passed on the news.

After collecting the engine kit and sweat cloths, my mate and I crossed the main line to the running shed. The six roads outside were empty, apart from the 'brand new' 4-6-0 in No 2 road. Judging by the black reek issuing from the chimney, the engine had been hauled out of the shed 'to get the air about it'. *Chamois*, as the saying went, was 'as cauld as a snawba'.

Viewing the engine at close range, I could see the smoke-filled cab with tongues of flame leaping from the firebox to ignite the escaping gases, forbidding the approach of the crew. The new paintwork was streaked with oil and coal dust, while traces of priming could be seen around the dome. There was steam at the anti-vacuum valve behind the chimney and the whistle was 'tuning up'.

'Do what you can with that lot, George,' I told my mate. 'I'm going for oil.' A cursory glance at the motion told me most of the oil corks were missing and I could see steam escaping from a mud door. This was not uncommon when an engine came off boiler washing, as obviously '1029 had. The corks would have been pinched by a driver too lazy to go to the proper place and the leaking mud door was the responsibility of the boilersmith, whom I advised on my way to the oil store. Reaching the serving hatch at this dispensary I banged the cans down and called out: '1029 – Carlisle!' This rudely awakened the slumbering storeman, who hobbled to the hatch and took the two cans – one for engine oil and one for cylinder oil. I looked round the corner of the hatch and watched the storeman labouring to turn the upright oil pump handle – one full turn for every pint and a full turn backwards in preparation for more pumping. 'Fill them up,' I called out, 'and get ready for the same again – I'll be back for more.' But the mournful 'chemist' only gave me the approved quantity, governed by

distance and the type of locomotive. To obtain the extra oil I knew I would require I had to get a 'chit' from the running foreman – a mere formality – but corks were there for the taking, so I took plenty, and gauge glasses, too.

On my return to the 'B1' I could see my mate had been busy. There was enough steam to operate the blower and the cab was free of smoke. The whole engine – inside and out – had been washed down with a water hosebag borrowed from the boiler washer. *Chamois* was approachable.

Had I been preparing a 3-cylinder locomotive I would have donned old overalls but one did not have to venture far under a 2-cylinder 'B1' and precautions against excessive dirt were unnecessary. All I had to oil were the outside motions, tender axleboxes and bogie axleboxes. In the cab were the oil feeds for the driving axlebox cheeks; the mechanical lubricators serving the axleboxes themselves and the cylinders were outside, on the footplate at the driver's side. The 'B1' was an easy locomotive for the driver to prepare, even in adverse circumstances as in this case.

When I returned with the extra oil for the lubricators, which were always on full feed for an ex-works locomotive, my mate was filling the tank and watering the coal, a load of local Whitehill fuel. There were huge lumps to be broken of this very hard coal, which tended to break into slices. At last I was able to climb into the cab and remove my serge jacket. Without thinking I hung it on a hook near the driving seat; normally this garment went into the big food box on the tender, along with my 'piece'. My choice of wardrobe that day was to prove handy later on. By this time, *Chamois* was on the boil and looking good. The warm air was heavy with the smell of fresh paint and newly-upholstered seats.

After testing the vacuum brake and injectors, we alerted the signalman to our readiness, then my mate made an 'injector brew' of tea – water from the injector in a syrup tin, boiled in seconds on the fire. Soon the 'B1' was striding out to Portobello. It was like sitting in a trap behind a prancing pony – the 6ft 2in driving wheels turning at speed carried us forward quickly and smoothly, while the four soft exhaust beats echoed as would hoof beats on turf. Approaching Portobello East Junction under clear

Above left:
'The six roads outside were empty, apart from the 4-6-0 . . .' but the description 'brand new' can hardly be applied to No 61344! *R. J. Sumner*

Left:
The 16.10 Edinburgh Waverley–Hawick restarts from Portobello in the charge of No 61350. *R. C. Nelson*

signals, I pushed down the pendulum steam regulator handle and coasted beneath the long signalbox astride the main line to beyond the yard signal at the entrance to the Waverley Route. Four 'shorts' on the whistle coincided with the signal being pulled off and *Chamois* glided backwards over points and crossings towards our train.

The fireman was coupling on and attending to the headcode lamps when the guard came along with details of the load and the number of braked vehicles on this partially-fitted freight. 'I'm ready when you are, driver,' he said, at which I gave a long blast on the whistle. As the signals ahead cleared, the yard foreman was there urging me on so that his 'N15' shunting engines could get back to work. Because of the twists and curves between the yard and the main line, the exchange of signals with the guard was not immediate but eventually George indicated to me that the train was following in the proper manner, with the guard in his wee caboose.

On the straight through Millerhill, with the reverser wound up to advantage and the piston valves on short travel, our speed increased as *Chamois*, on full throttle, beat out a rapid tattoo. As I gazed out over the great marshalling yard that is Millerhill, George, too, was getting into his stride, lashing coal into the hungry flames, striving for the super heat that would take us over Falahill, 880ft above sea level.

Up we went through Hardengreen where assisting engines were available when required. These had the reputation of being 'hangers on'; from the sanctuary of collery sidings I have seen long freight trains labouring on the incline with 75 tons of 'J36' hanging on behind – the coupling tight, the driver and fireman having a chat. After crossing the great South Esk viaduct we were passing Fushiebridge and nearing the 1 in 70 gradient, the last stage of the climb to Falahill. By this time the fire was heavy and *Chamois* was tiring, so I let out

Above:
'On the straight through Millerhill . . .' No 61354 gets
into its stride with a stopping train for Hawick on 5
September 1963. *Derek Cross*

Left:
Chamois itself heads a Kingmoor–Edinburgh freight
at Carnwath, on the Clyde Valley line from Carstairs.
Derek Cross

the reverser into full forward gear and we
approached the summit in style.

From his lonely outpost at Falahill the signalman
waved us on, indicating clear signals ahead. George
laid his shovel aside and relaxed to the sound of the
singing injector filling the boiler. The countryside
was really beautiful that spring morning as sheep
and lambs in nearby fields ran away from an
antelope in full flight. On this stretch the twisting
railway crossed an equally winding Gala Water
fourteen times and, looking back along the
irregular vehicles of the train, I saw in my
imagination a wriggling snake with hiccups. Soon I
was braking for the permanent speed restrictions at
Bowshank Tunnel and as we entered this damp
cavern there was one mighty explosion in the cab.

A bursting gauge glass is always a frightening
experience. Although one immediately realises the
cause of the explosion, that in no way diminishes
the seriousness of the problem on a moving
locomotive. All the way downhill *Chamois* had
been on 'cushion' steam, the regulator valve just off
the face, and fortunately when the glass burst our
speed was not great. Leaving the controls I quickly
grabbed my jacket, put it over my head and felt my
way towards the left-hand gauge column where
steam under great pressure was seeking an outlet
behind thick glass protectors.

9

The top steam key was difficult to operate because of its newness but after some persuasion and burnt knuckles the flow of steam was checked. The lower key came up to the horizontal position more readily and soon the gauge column was isolated and the cab clear of steam and water. Somewhat exhausted – and soaked to the skin – I returned to my driving seat. In the well of the cab (aptly named, I thought!) my mate stood drenched and looking very dejected while the heat of the fire raised steam from his sodden clothes.

But we exchanged a grin, to indicate that all was well, and as I leaned out of the side window I could see the smokebox nameplate, *Chamois*, gleaming in the sunshine. This time I smiled to myself. *I* felt like an unwrung chamois leather! Yet all is now forgiven and I would be proud to find a place in my home for that nameplate.

Above right:
Near Newcastleton on 5 June 1965, 'B1' No 61349 begins the nine-mile ascent at 1 in 75 to Whitrope with an Edinburgh-bound Waveley Route freight.
W. J. V. Anderson

Right:
Just a few yards from where the gauge glass of *Chamois* burst, the 'Granite City' railtour emerges from Bowshank Tunnel in the opposite direction on 3 September 1966. Heading the train is the Scottish Region's last 'V2' 2-6-2 No 60836 – which was to become the last of the class withdrawn from service at the end of that year. *G. Kinghorn*

Below:
One of No 61029's more numerous African antelope 'cousins', No 61007 *Klipspringer* heads an Edinburgh Waverley–Carlisle train at Riddings Junction on 16 April 1953. *H. C. Casserley*

Between Peterborough and Leicester

A 50-mile rural link between the fringe of East Anglia and the East Midlands, forming part of a cross-country passenger route and seeing a variety of freight traffic – that's the line between Peterborough and Leicester, shown in pictures on the next few pages.

Below:
Most of the passenger services on the line are provided by Birmingham–Cambridge/Norwich trains. At Helpston, in the pouring rain on 17 December 1983, Class 31 No 31.410 has just begun to run parallel to the ECML which it will follow for the next six miles to Peterborough with the 10.15 Birmingham New Street–Norwich. *John C. Baker*

Left:
Class 47 No 47.457 heads the summer Saturdays 09.28 Norwich–Birmingham past Uffington signalbox on 16 June 1984. The station here, Uffington & Barnack, closed in 1952. *J. Checkley*

Centre left:
Approaching Stamford on 21 February 1984, Class 25s Nos 25.250 and 25.300 are in charge of a Mountsorrel–Kennett 'Redland' stone train. *John Rudd*

Below left:
A Ratcliffe–Fletton fly-ash train, headed by '45' No 45.041 *Royal Tank Regiment,* passes Luffenham Junction on 21 February 1984. *John Rudd*

Below:
The tail of an eastbound fly-ash train passes the brake van of a rake of Peterborough–Toton unfitted coal empties, hauled by Class 20s Nos 20.186 and 20.170 at Manton Junction on 16 August 1983. The line on the right leads to Corby and joins the Midland main line at Glendon Junction. *John Chalcraft*

Bottom:
A Class 105 DMU on an extra working passes the site of Ashwell station on 21 April 1983. *John C. Baker*

Above:
An up empty tank train passes Ashwell on 21 April 1983 behind Class 47 No 47.104. *John C. Baker*

Top right:
Diverted from the Midland main line on 21 April 1983, the 13.30 Sheffield—St Pancras IC125 passes Ashwell. *John C. Baker*

Right:
Class 31 No 31.410 and the 07.40 Norwich—Birmingham head through the winter landscape near Whissendine on 6 January 1984. *John C. Baker*

Above:
Heading the 11.00 Corby–Toton special air-braked service on 17 April 1984, '58' No 58.004 passes the site of Saxby station, closed in 1961. *John A. Day*

Below:
Now one of only three stations open between Peterborough and Leicester (the others are Stamford and Oakham), Melton Mowbray on 23 February 1984 sees '25' No 25.173 trundling through with the 11.21 Wards Sidings–Castle Bromwich cement. *A. Wynn*

Above:
The tall Melton station signalbox looks down on Class 45 No 45.033 and an eastbound freight on 23 February 1984. *A. Wynn*

Below:
Another station closed in 1961 was Frisby, where a Class 120 diesel unit is seen on 21 April 1983 forming the 08.23 Birmingham–Peterborough. *John C. Baker*

Above:
Class 56 No 56.010 at Kirby Bellars, near Melton Mowbray, with the 13.00 Toton-Northfleet MGR on 23 February 1984. *A. Wynn*

Below:
A westbound ballast train is headed by '37' No 37.076 near Frisby on 21 April 1983. *John C. Baker*

A New Twist to a Familiar Tale

Alex Rankin

The story of the two bridges across the Forth and Tay has been often told, particularly the disaster which befell the first Tay Bridge. Not generally known is that there were two attempts at bridging the Firth of Forth.

There had been very early plans for bridges across the Forth but these went no further than the completion of drawings. The earliest was for a slender suspension bridge, drawn up in 1818 to carry road traffic. In 1864 a bridge was proposed by the North British Railway for a viaduct from Blackness Castle to Charlestown. This viaduct proceeded as far as borings being taken. It was found that the river bed was unsuitable and the project was abandoned.

In the next few years the focus of attention moved to Dundee and the Tay Bridge. Thomas Bouch had dreamed of spanning both firths since 1849 and drew up plans for the two bridges simultaneously. Three Bills for a Tay Bridge were put forward in the 1860s and the Royal Assent was given on 15 July 1870. The foundation stone was laid on 22 July 1870.

Meantime, Bouch had been preparing for his magnum opus – a twin suspension bridge with the two tracks 120ft apart. The towers were to be 550ft high and the 1,600ft spans gave a maximum of 150ft headroom at high tide. A company was set up with a capital of £1,666,666, guaranteed by the Midland, North Eastern and Great Northern Railways, as well as the North British Railway; this was the Forth Bridge Railway Co and its incorporation received the Royal Assent on 5 August 1873. Work did not begin until 1877/78 when contracts were let to

Below:
The classic view of the Forth Bridge, with 'A3' Pacific No 60052 *Prince Palatine* heading a Dundee–Edinburgh train on 17 July 1965. *K. Hale*

Messrs John Waddell. The first pillar was constructed and the ceremony of laying the foundation stone took place.

Then, on 28 December 1879, the Tay Bridge was blown down in a gale with the loss of a passenger train and its occupants. All work on the Forth Bridge stopped. The report on the disaster was published on 4 August 1880 but the contracts had already been cancelled. A Bill for full abandonment was laid before Parliament in 1880/81. The three English railway companies objected but, before the Bill was debated, it was replaced by a Bill for a new bridge. This was passed in 1882; the bridge was completed in 1889 and opened in March 1890. The pillar for the earlier suspension bridge is still there today, beneath the centre cantilever of the present bridge, and carries a navigation light beacon.

Below:
A Metro-Cammell DMU, forming the 10.15 Edinburgh–Dundee on 28 May 1977, passes a plaque commemorating the official opening of the Forth Bridge by the Prince of Wales on 4 March 1890.
Brian Morrison

Right:
Freight trains hauled by a Class J38 0-6-0 (approaching) and a Class K2 2-6-0 pass on one of the cantilever sections in early BR days. *E. R. Wethersett*

The Forth Bridge Railway Co operated from Dalmeny South Junction across the bridge to Inverkeithing South Junction. Train services were worked by the North British Railway although, according to an agreement of 1869, the North Eastern possessed running powers to Perth. Needless to say, these were never exercised although, in later pre-Grouping years, NER Atlantics ran to Glasgow. One NER locomotive known to have crossed the bridge was a 'T3' (later LNER 'Q7') 0-8-0, en route for tests on Glenfarg Bank in 1921. The Midland Railway ran through coaches over NBR metals to Inverness via Edinburgh and Perth. In 1923 its share of the Forth Bridge Railway Co passed to the LMS, while the remainder was taken over by the LNER. During World War 2 certain LMS locomotives worked over the bridge but normally that company's share was limited to the through coach workings. The Forth Bridge Railway Co remained in existence until, with the rest of the main line system, it was nationalised and became part of British Railways on 1 January 1948. Its fare structure had allowed a toll charge covering 19 miles, levied on its share holding companies and, today, fares across the bridge are slightly higher than normal.

The company had its own legal standing which, in the 1930s and 1940s, was handled by the LNER from its Marylebone office. Strangely enough, I have not seen its registered seal featured in a railway publication. This dated from the Bill of 1873 and was an interesting item because it showed the original suspension bridge design. Being a legally registered seal of authority it could not be changed and thus remained in use until the end of 1947! Ironically a suspension bridge did eventually span the Firth of Forth at Queensferry but that was 90 years after the original proposal and was designed for motor cars – something unheard of in 1873 when the seal was made.

Right:
After Nationalisation, ex-LMS locomotives were more frequently seen crossing the Forth Bridge. 'Jubilee' 4-6-0 No 45692 *Cyclops* enters Dalmeny station on 15 June 1957 with a parcels service from Perth. *David A. Anderson*

Above:
The Aberdeen portion of the 11.00 from King's Cross passes Forth Bridge North signalbox and approaches North Queensferry in June 1964, hauled by an English Electric Type 4. *W. J. V. Anderson*

Below:
With the road bridge in the background a Derby three-car DMU rumbles along the last few yards of the Forth Bridge at North Queensferry on 7 May 1966. *C. T. Gifford*

Some Nasmyth Wilson Survivors

Thomas Worsley and Geoffrey Hill

Few travellers visit India without stopping at Bombay, the Gateway to India. For many it is the introduction to this hospitable land of contrasts and of steam. Apart from the pilots at Parel Locomotive Works (Central Railway), no Indian Railways steam locomotives are to be seen in the neighbourhood of Bombay. But a few miles north on the electrified suburban lines from the great oriental gothic Victoria Terminus – a station which makes St Pancras look like a matchstick model – are the lines of the Bombay Port Trust which see regular steam working. As many as a dozen 2-6-0Ts are steamed each day at Wadala shed and share duties on the Port Trust lines with a rather larger number of diesel shunters. Some 10 of the surviving

2-6-0Ts are Nasmyth Wilson-built and most still carry the distinctive triangular works plate on the cabside, as well as a large brass crest on the bunker displaying the intertwined initials and name of the owner. A bridge north of Wadala station provides an excellent vantage point. Even on a Sunday afternoon when the lines tend to be quieter, Nos 20 and 24 (NW 1364 and 1368 of 1921) were found double-heading a freight from the Port Trust lines

Below:
Broad gauge (5ft 6in) Bombay Port Trust 2-6-0Ts Nos 20 and 24 reverse a freight into Wadala exchange sidings, Bombay, on 21 November 1982.
T. E. Worsley

to the exchange sidings with Indian Railways in November 1982. An immaculate No 16 (NW 1360 of 1921) was shunting in a nearby yard.

A night's journey from Bombay on the Central Railway line through Pune towards Wadi and the South Central Railway brings the enthusiast to Kurdawadi, the centre of the 2ft 6in gauge system that was once the independent Barsi Light Railway. Extending for 190km to Miraj in the southwest and 137km via Barsi Town to Latur in the northeast, this line must have the largest collection of active Nasmyth Wilson locomotives in the world. Two types, the 'F' class 2-8-2s and the 'G' class 4-6-4s, predominate; they are supplemented by two post-war standard 'ZE' 2-8-2s which are too heavy for much of the main line track and are mainly employed on station pilot work. Ten of the 13 'Fs', Nos 712-721, and seven of the nine 'Gs', Nos 725/6 and 728-32, are Nasmyth built. After the demise of the Patricroft firm, later additions to the 'F' class came from Hunslet and to the 'G' class from Bagnall. As is so common on Indian railways, none of these locomotives carries a works plate – presumably they were removed and melted down into brass water pots long ago! There are usually at least half a dozen engines in steam on shed at Kurdawadi at any time and a further 10 or so out on the line.

During the hours of daylight Kurdawadi sees departures on both lines, early morning and late afternoon. These occur almost simultaneously and the photographer has to be lucky or athletic to record both of them, as the Latur and Miraj lines separate only a few yards from the platform ends. There is a further mid-morning mixed train to Barsi Town, returning in the heat of the afternoon, and in the late morning trains arrive from Latur and Pandharpur, a pilgrimage centre on the Miraj line. Both 'F' and 'G' classes work passenger trains, with freights tending to be monopolised by the 2-8-2s.

During our last visit, in November 1982, we learned of the impending arrival of two diesel locomotives for trials but a footplate ride on 'F' class 2-8-2 No 720 to Barsi Town and back confirmed the shedmaster's assertion that the Nasmyths are in good order and should see several more years of service.

Murtajapur, on the Central Railway line between Bhusaval and Nagpur, provides a home for two Nasmyth locomotives of the 2ft 6in gauge 'B1' class, built for the Great Indian Peninsular Railway in 1926. The North British Locomotive Co supplied five earlier examples of this class, all of which are at Murtajapur together with six postwar Japanese-built 'ZD' 2-8-2s and a lone 'BS' class 2-8-2. In December 1980, 'B/1' No 771 was observed working as yard pilot; the shed foreman had one of its building plates, polished and mounted, kept safely in his desk.

A handful of Nasmyth locomotives remain active on the extensive South Eastern Railway 2ft 6in gauge system known as the Satpura lines from Jabalpur in the north, via Nainpur and Nagbhir link with a more westerly section from Chhindwara to Nagpur. Including several shorter branches, this narrow gauge system extends to just over 1,000km. There are engine sheds at Nagpur (Motibagh), Chhindwara, Nainpur and Gondia. At Motibagh shed in November 1980 we found 2-8-2 No 658 (Nasmyth Wilson 1017 of 1913), one of the last surviving 'BC' class, a variant of the earlier 'B' class converted to superheat. The separate classification is retained although the 'BC' class is virtually indistinguishable from the more numerous 'BS' class which was superheated from new. Nasmyth 'BS' No 632 (NW 1371 of 1922) was fresh from works and undergoing a steam test.

Left:
In immaculate condition, No 16 shunts at Wadala on 21 November 1982. Note the Bombay Port Trust crest on the bunker and the triangular builders' plate on the cabside. *T. E. Worsley*

Below:
Somewhat overcrowded – by British standards, at least – the 16.00 mixed train for Latur leaves Kurdawadi on 7 December 1980. In charge is former Barsi Light Railway, now Central Railway, 2ft 6in gauge 'G' class 4-6-4 No 728 (Nasmyth Wilson 1539/built 1928). *T. E. Worsley*

Most trains on the western and southern sections are diesel powered, although a long line of derelict diesels at Nagpur ensured that steam was used on a number of workings. Further east the 228km Gondia–Jabalpur section was almost entirely steam worked at the time of our visit. Much of the traffic was in the hands of standard 'ZE' 2-8-2s with a few 'BS' 2-8-2s retained for shunting and local freight. At Nainpur in November 1982, 'BS' No 636 (NW 1375 of 1922) was shunting in the goods yard and No 613 of the same class (NW 1087 of 1915) was under repair. Only the first two 'ZEs' came from Britain (NW 1531 and 1532 of 1928); during our visit we found the first of these, now Indian Railways No 93, looking somewhat woebegone awaiting repair at Gondia. The rest of this large class were supplied by French, German and Japanese builders over many years ending in the 1950s.

Ranchi, in the southern corner of the state of Bihar, one of India's most populous and least prosperous regions, provides another home for the 'BS' and 'BC' classes on the 2ft 6in gauge. Fourteen are allocated to this South Eastern Railway depot, of which six are Nasmyths, the others coming from North British and the Yorkshire Engine Co. Two North British 'CC' class 4-6-2s are allocated for passenger workings although a 'BS' takes over if a 'CC' is unavailable. One 'BS' is outstationed on the now isolated Purulia–Kotshila section.

Bauxite is the main traffic on the 69km line from Ranchi to Lohardaga. In December 1982 there were three workings a day, two of which were double-headed, thus Ranchi provides another opportunity to see these Lancashire-built engines in harness. Morning and evening passenger trains also run in each direction. The line is hilly with some fine bridges and passes through country largely inaccessible by road. A ride out to Lohardaga and back on the passenger train, some 3½hr each way, was an enjoyable day out and provided many opportunities for photography at wayside stations and at a water stop by a river bridge a few miles short of Lohardaga. As is so common on Indian steam railways, a friendly approach to the driver and the gift of some photographs resulted in a warm welcome into the cab for a footplate ride.

To complete this survey, mention should be made of two other Nasmyth classes which have been taken out of service in recent years. The first is the delightful little 2ft 6in gauge 'RD' class 2-6-2, Nos 687–90. These machines were built in 1929 (works numbers 1563–66) for service on the Raipur to Dhamtari and Rajim lines of the South Eastern Railway. Increasing traffic led to their replacement by larger (and older) locomotives of the 'CC' class, but, fortunately, one has been retained for preservation at Raipur and another at Nagpur Works.

Top:
Almost everyone poses for the camera at Chinkhill on 22 November 1982! Heading the 09.00 Kurdawadi–Barsi Town mixed train is Central Railway (ex-Barsi Light Railway) 'F' 2-8-2 No 720 (NW 1575/1929).
T. E. Worsley

Above:
Built by Nasmyth Wilson for the Great Indian Peninsular Railway, 'B/1' 2-8-2 No 771 (NW 1488/1926) shunts a Japanese-built 'ZD' 2-8-2 and water carriers at the Central Railway Murtajapur shed on 5 December 1980. *T. E. Worsley*

Finally it is now probably too late to see a member of the 'T' class metre gauge 2-6-2Ts which formerly operated from Lucknow (Charbagh) shed. Six were built by Nasmyths in 1937 (works Nos 1643–48) and others came from Bagnall. These locomotives performed shunting and pilot duties at Lucknow but have been withdrawn in recent times. The likelihood must be that they have now been cut up.

Nasmyth hunting in India is highly recommended and affords the opportunity to see British-built locomotives at work over a large area of the sub-continent against a fascinating variety of largely rural surroundings. Provided he is armed with permission for photography from the Ministry of Railways, the visiting enthusiast is assured of very warm hospitality from railwaymen of all grades. One driver on the metre gauge, delighted with the gift of some black-and-white prints of the 'YP' Pacifics he drove, told us we had been 'sent by God'. When did that last happen to you on an Inter-City 125?

Nasmyth Wilson & Co

Nasmyth's Bridgewater Foundry at Patricroft, Manchester, was opened in 1836 by James and George Nasmyth. In 1838 a Mr Gaskell joined the brothers and the firm became known as Nasmyth Gaskell & Co. James Nasmyth was a versatile engineer, most famous for his invention of the steam hammer in 1839, the year in which the company's first locomotive was built. The company went through several changes of name in the next few years, the final style of Nasmyth Wilson & Co being adopted in 1867.

In excess of 1,600 locomotives were built between 1839 and the end of the company's existence in 1938 but only just over 200 were for the home market. Some lasted well into the 1950s, including five 'Tilbury' 4-4-2Ts for the LMS, 12 Taff Vale 'A' class 0-6-2Ts and a number of 'ROD' 2-8-0s. One batch of Nasmyth locomotives lasted until the 1960s; these were the 10 0-4-4Ts of Caledonian Railway design built for the LMS, which eventually became BR Nos 55260-69. A small number of industrial locomotives was also built for home use.

In excess of one third of the company's total output – indeed, most locomotives built in the last two decades of the company's existence – were built for Indian railways. With one exception, all the broad gauge (5ft 6in) and metre gauge types have disappeared in the face of dieselisation, electrification and standardisation on a small number of steam classes. On the narrow gauge (2ft 6in) lines about 35 of the company's products, representing six classes, survived at the beginning of 1983.

Right:
'BS' 2-8-2s Nos 619 (NW 1094/1915) and 635 (NW 1374/1922) cross the broad gauge lines at Ranchi on 3 December 1982 with a bauxite train from Lohardaga. *T. E. Worsley*

Below right:
At Ranchi on 3 December 1982, 'BS' 2-8-2 No 617 (NW 1092/1915) reverses a bauxite train prior to unloading into the broad gauge wagons beneath. *T. E. Worsley*

Below:
South Eastern Railway 'BS' 2-8-2 No 636 at Nainpur on 25 November 1982. *T. E. Worsley*

25 Years of Irish Railways

Michael H. C. Baker

Railway anniversaries seem to be a feature of the 1980s. One of the more significant of 1984 marked 150 years of railways in Ireland. There was also the rather less significant one of my own 25 years of visiting and at times living in that country. Looking back over a quarter century, many memories and images come to mind, some of times and people gone for good, some seemingly unchanged and others brought back by the growing preservation scene.

One of the pleasures and, occasionally discomforts, of an Irish visit is the getting there. August 1984 saw us embarking at Stranraer, having watched with some astonishment the vast numbers of customers disgorging from the candy-striped carriages of the Glasgow boat train. I never take this route without a wobble of apprehension, recalling the fate of one of the earliest car ferries, the *Princess Victoria* which sank with considerable loss of life en route from Stranraer to Larne in a gale on 31 January 1953. Ship design has changed greatly since those days and this, the shortest of the Irish Sea routes, carries an enormous traffic, particularly freight. Sadly, despite harbour stations on both sides, freight traffic is mainly carried by road.

I need have had no fear, for the conditions were millpond-like. We watched a three-car DEMU arrive at Larne Harbour station from Belfast under LMS design semaphores (where I had as late as 1969 seen a Derby designed 2-6-4T in charge of a rake of LMS wooden-bodied carriages) and then drove south to Dublin. Arriving in the capital of the Republic soon after dark we caught a glimpse of the bright lights of a DART electric unit running alongside Dublin Bay. I had to contain myself and wait until next morning to ride in the most exciting development in Irish transport in all my years of travel in that country.

The ghost of the great Jim Larkin, joint founder with James Connolly of the Irish trade union movement, whose statue now stands in O'Connell

Below:
Modern CIE freight. At Malahide on 23 August 1984 the 13.31 Dublin–Belfast freightliner passes the 13.40 Platin (Drogheda)–North Wall (Dublin) cement train. The latter is hauled by Class 201 Bo-Bo No 222, one of the Metropolitan Vickers diesels introduced in the mid-1950s and now fitted with General Motors engines. *Michael H. C. Baker*

Street, must surely have been smiling this summer for it was he who, in the first decade of this century, suggested electrifying the Dublin suburban railways. Commuter services 25 years ago were a mixture of steam and diesel and losing out both to the buses and private cars. One line, from Harcourt Street to Bray, had just been closed and things generally were at a low ebb. The second Bray line, from Amiens Street and Westland Row, was worked largely by Coras Iompair Eireann AEC/Park Royal railcars, whilst the Great Northern lines to Howth and Drogheda employed a mixture of similar railcars and steam-hauled trains in the charge of 4-4-2Ts, 4-4-0s and 0-6-0s.

Actually the GNR had ceased to exist over a year earlier, in 1956, but much of its rolling stock still bore the original colours. It had long been the most highly regarded of the Irish railways, both by the general public and the enthusiast fraternity (a small but discerning group in Ireland). Like all Irish railways it had fallen on hard times in the 1930s, although it pursued petrol and diesel railcar development as one way out of its difficulties. The revival of its fortunes during the war encouraged it to order ten 4-4-0s immediately afterwards, the very last locomotives of that wheel arrangement built for use in the western world. Both types, elegant as were all GNR 4-4-0s, were at work in Dublin in 1959. With the dissolution of the GNR they had been divided up between CIE and the Ulster Transport Authority. The smaller class, the 'U', essentially a 1915 design, could be seen on stopping trains, but although diesel railcars had taken over many of the Dublin-Belfast workings there was still some work left for steam. On the last evening of my visit I had the good fortune to be at Amiens Street when the heavy 5pm non-stop Belfast express, composed entirely of GNR carriages in their original mahogany livery, pulled out behind the high stepping 'VS' 4-4-0 No 58 *Lagan*. Designed by H. McIntosh and built by Beyer Peacock in 1948 she looked quite splendid with her almost Duchess-proportioned boiler, smoke deflectors, long wheelbase and Caledonian blue livery with black and white lining.

Two years later I came across her again at her home shed of Adelaide, Belfast, and even managed to travel as far as Dundalk behind steam, though not in the charge of a GNR 4-4-0. We had one of the UTA 2-6-4Ts which were destined to become the last main line steam locomotives at work in the British Isles, outlasting everything on British Rail.

Steam generally lasted longer on the northern lines than in the south, which was fine for the enthusiast. But beyond this it was a reflection of different attitudes in the six and 26 counties to the role of railways. In the long term there was nothing very complimentary you could say about the former. Branch lines were closing, as were many rural and suburban stations on the main lines and even some main lines looked pretty insecure. But at least in the Republic there was a commitment to the future of a basic railway system. Following the introduction of railcars on both express and local workings in the early 1950s there had been a veritable flood of diesel-electric locomotives which by 1959 had removed steam from all but a few relatively minor duties.

These diesels were not particularly impressive looking machines, a state of affairs compounded by their sombre livery – green, silver or black, relieved by nothing other than large quantities of spilt oil and accumulated grime. For all that, most of them

Below:
A Northern Ireland Railways Class 80 DMU arrives at Larne from Belfast on 11 August 1984.
Michael H. C. Baker

are still around today and both looking and performing a good deal better than in what was supposed to be their prime.

Such, then, was the scene in 1959.

In 1984 not all was sweetness and light and CIE was running a massive deficit in an economy which was under severe strain, but nevertheless there was much to gladden the soul. A heartening change of attitude in the north, at least partly brought about by the realisation that some of the strains and erupting tensions of that hard-pressed community are due to decades – some might say centuries – of economic neglect, has meant a good deal of investment in railways. Lines and stations have been reopened and much new rolling stock has been put into service, whilst the remarkable achievements of the Railway Preservation Society of Ireland, which has its headquarters at Whitehead on the Larne-Belfast line, has received much official recognition and encouragement.

In the south, two events illuminated a year which might otherwise have been rather downbeat. One was the long awaited entry into service of the BREL designed Mk 3 main line carriages. By August sufficient had been completed for them to operate three return workings between Dublin and Cork each weekday. This batch arrived fully-assembled from Derby but more were being assembled when I visited Inchicore Works and the later examples of the total order of 124 carriages were to be put together by CIE from pre-cut plates and frames. One of the chief variations from BR operated Mk 3s is their swing plug doors which struck me as a pretty silly extravagance for a railway which is hard pressed financially. They had already caused delays through failure to operate properly and had given a few headaches to the engineering staff at Inchicore. But otherwise the new carriages are a most handsome addition to CIE's main line fleet, which has been desperately short of both main line and suburban rolling stock for some years.

Which brings me to the remarkable DARTs. It is no exaggeration to say they were the talk of Dublin last summer and not merely amongst commuters and the railway fraternity. Amongst the down-and-outs by the Quays, listening to the idle banter of Gaelic football crowds on their way to Croke Park, at smart cocktail parties in Dalkey, one was bound to hear sooner rather than later: '. . . and have you travelled on the DART yet?'

After years of suffering the vagaries of the old push and pulls which should have been given a decent burial years ago, July 1984 saw the inauguration of the Dublin Area Rapid Transit system, 38km and £113 million worth of double track electrified railway from Bray in the south to Howth on the north edge of Dublin Bay. Everyone, it seemed, wanted to take a ride on the sleek, smooth green EMUs running at a headway of between six and 20 minutes from around 7am to midnight Monday to Saturday and almost as frequently on Sundays. I several times travelled in the cab of a DART and found it uncanny that the acceleration, speed and braking was virtually taken out of the driver's control and put in the charge of the computerised operations centre. It was enormously impressive but I wondered how the drivers themselves felt about the change in their status. None was prepared to commit himself unequivocally, for the system had been working only a few weeks. At the end of the trial period they had to make up their minds whether to stay on the DARTs or go back to locomotive operated non-suburban working. CIE argue that however vigilant drivers are they will inevitably become so dependent on the automatic signalling that it would be dangerous suddenly to deprive them of this and put them back to visual signalling systems. A number of drivers could see the logic of this although at least one vehemently disagreed and most persuasively put the case for relieving what might possibly become the monotony of being little better than an opener and closer of doors. I was somewhat amused by one driver with whom I was travelling on the northern section of DART territory approaching Howth Junction. It is an area of recent, extensive and pretty miserable looking high density housing development where there is much unemployment and a good deal of vandalism. I had been impressed with the complete absence of graffiti on the trains and asked how this was achieved. We had some fairly lively, likely-looking lads aboard. 'Watch,' he said as we drew into the station. The doors slid open and a man with a large

Left:
Ulster Transport Authority (ex-GNR) Class VS 4-4-0 No 58 *Lagan* **pulls out of Dublin Amiens Street (now Connolly) in September 1959 with the 5pm for Belfast.** *Michael H. C. Baker*

alsatian got in. A deathly hush descended upon the customers and most got out at the next stop. 'Never fails,' said the driver. 'They'll take on half a dozen security men if they're in the mood but since we've introduced dog patrols, they're as well behaved as novice nuns.'

Apart from DARTs and main line CIE expresses I travelled quite extensively on Northern Ireland Railways last summer, sampling the various types of DEMUs which work the stopping services throughout the system and practically all trains on the Portrush and Derry line, and also the ex-BR Mk 2s which are employed on the Dublin-Belfast expresses, powered by the big, handsome General Motors 2,250hp Co-Cos. The new station at Newry, just across the border, seemed to be doing excellent business as did the numerous suburban stations on the southern approach to Belfast. Vandalism, bombing and neglect means that some of them were pretty miserable looking affairs, but Lisburn maintained much of its Great Northern character, complete with semaphore signals (though these were about to be replaced with colour lights), and the new Belfast Central is very fine.

I also rode behind steam on the narrow gauge Shane's Castle Railway, a delightful experience rumbling through the woods down to the shores of Lough Derg, the largest inland piece of water in the British Isles, initially in a former Belgian tramcar and later, as the day improved, in an open toastrack. Even better and at long last, I managed a trip in the RPSI's preserved train, from Drogheda to Dublin behind 2-6-4T No 4, the very same locomotive I had photographed right at the end of regular steam in Ireland, at Larne in 1969. I made the most of the opportunity, sampling the riding of former NCC, Great Northern, Great Southern & Western, and Great Southern carriages as the packed and extremely convivial train steamed south on its way from Belfast to Dublin. The RPSI operates over both CIE and NIR tracks, draws members and its spendid collection of rolling stock from both sides of the border and does a marvellous public relations job for tourism, especially in the north. Would that the community at large in that part of the world took to its heart the RPSI's shining example of how to make friends and live at peace with their neighbours.

Below:
CIE railcar No 2650 passes East Wall Junction, Dublin, en route for Howth in August 1964. Some of these railcars, dating from the early 1950s, were later converted to push-pull vehicles for use on Dublin suburban workings and have now been superseded by the Dublin Area Rapid Transit (DART) electric service. *Michael H. C. Baker*

Bottom:
In the predominantly black CIE livery of the time, General Motors Bo-Bo No B144 is on freight duty in August 1974 at Castleisland on a now-closed branch in County Kerry. *Michael H. C. Baker*

Above :
**One of the DART two-car EMUs stands at Howth in
August 1984.** *Michael H. C. Baker*

Left:
**A tranquil scene on the Shane's Castle Railway,
featuring former Bord na Mona 0-4-0WT No 3** *Shane.*
Michael H. C. Baker

Below:
**Steam, diesel and electric at Dublin Connolly in
August 1984 – represented by the RPSI's former NCC
2-6-4T No 4, CIE Class 001 Co-Co No 030 and a DART
electric unit. On the left, two push-pull trains await
their next duty.** *Michael H. C. Baker*

Shortly before electrification work commenced, Class 141 Bo-Bo No 169 heads a Dublin—Bray train round Dublin Bay.   *M. Floate*

Below:
A four-car DART at Bray on 31 August 1984 with a Class 201 Bo-Bo on one of the push-pull trains in the background.   *Colin Boocock*

Postal Portraits

Top left:
The 15.45 Aberdeen portion of the up 'West Coast Postal' approaches Craiginches Yard on 28 August 1984 behind Class 47 No 47.467. *D. M. May*

Left:
Until October 1982, the 20.15 King's Cross—Edinburgh conveyed passenger accommodation. Now much reduced in length, the train passes Oakleigh Park behind Class 31 No 31.242 on 5 July 1983. *David Percival*

Top right:
Catching the last rays of the setting sun on 25 April 1984, the 19.27 Penzance—Paddington 'postal' sets out on its journey behind Class 50 No 50.043 *Eagle*. *Michael H. C. Baker*

Right:
Class 45 No 45.101 at Derby with three TPO vehicles which will be attached to the 17.35 Leeds—Bristol on 23 June 1981. *C. J. Tuffs*

PTE Colours on Rail

Above:
In Strathclyde livery (but outside the PTE-supported network), a Class 107 DMU forms a Glasgow–Stranraer service on 14 May 1984. *Neil Batteley*

Below:
A Class 114 unit in South Yorkshire colours on 3 April 1984, with additional embellishments to mark the 10th anniversary of the Passenger Transport Executive. *L. A. Nixon*

Two-in-One

Most railway photographers consider it a bonus to successfully capture two trains in one picture. Sometimes the result can be planned; more often, the opportunity occurs by chance and the photographer must make an instant decision on the composition. In this feature we see how various photographers have employed situations to their advantage.

Below left:
On busy Southern Region lines the oppportunity to photograph two trains together generally occurs more frequently than elsewhere. At East Croydon on 24 September 1983, 4-TEP EMU No 2701 passes a 4-VEP as it departs at the head of the 13.22 Victoria–Littlehampton. *Alex Dasi-Sutton*

Bottom left:
Where stationary trains are involved, the scene when one begins to move can be anticipated. Such was the case at Loughborough on 7 February 1983 when '37' No 37.046 departed on the 10.00 ballast working to York Yard North. Class 45 No 45.043 *Royal Inniskilling Fusilier* waits with a load destined for Healey Mills. *C. J. Tuffs*

Right:
By firing the shutter slightly earlier than was planned, the photographer made use of the unexpected DMU in his picture of Class 40 No 40.104 with the morning Stanlow–Hunslet oil tank train at Marsh Lane, Leeds, on 28 March 1984. *G. W. Morrison*

Below:
Two stationary trains (or four, counting the IC125 and rake of carriages!) at York on 9 March 1984. Class 31 No 31.428 has arrived with the 21.15 from Scarborough and '47' No 47.486 heads the 22.34 York–Shrewsbury mail. *C. L. Shaw*

Above:
IC125s on the 18.15 Nottingham—St Pancras and
18.15 St Pancras—Derby services meet, as scheduled,
at Kettering in June 1984. *W. A. Sharman*

Above:
Class 37 No 37.190 waits at Dalwhinnie to head northwards with a freight for Inverness on 25 July 1984 as the 07.20 Inverness–King's Cross 'Highland Chieftain' approaches. One of the IC125's second class trailers is unusually marshalled at the first class end of the formation next to leading power car No 43100 *Craigentinny*. *C. J. M. Lofthus*

Below:
Perhaps we should not give the game away by revealing the information that Class 31 No 31.180 was stationary! Nevertheless, careful composition was required as the 13.05 Richmond–Broad Street departed from Willesden Junction on 2 March 1984. *Richard Lyndsell*

Above:
Little room for manoeuvre here – precise firing of the shutter was essential. Class 56 No 56.116 stands at signals with empty MGR wagons in Horbury cutting on 22 February 1984 as Class 47 No 47.215 passes with ballast for Healey Mills. *John A. Day*

Below:
A Class 108 DMU approaches Bredbury on a New Mills–Manchester service on 25 April 1984 and passes a similar unit travelling in the opposite direction. *Steve Turner*

Above:
The 'bonus' is a Class 101 DMU standing in
Kidderminster station as Class 58 No 58.006 makes a
Bescot–Worcester crew training run on 6 June 1984.
On the left is the connection to the Severn Valley
Railway. *B. J. Robbins*

Below:
Even the photographer might admit that 'lady luck'
played her part at Southampton on 18 February 1984.
Class 33 No 33.035 with the late-running 13.10
Portsmouth Harbour–Bristol Temple Meads passes
No 33.018 with the 12.10 service in the reverse
direction. *Alex Dasi-Sutton*

43

Main Line Steam

The resurgence of steam traction on BR metals since the early 1970s has rekindled and generated interest amongst enthusiasts, railwaymen and the general public alike. Fortunately, locomotives of each of the 'big four' companies have been available for these duties, appearing in unfamiliar territory as well as working over routes on which they once performed.

Left:
Flying Scotsman passed this way many times in LNER and BR days, but rarely with a 'B1' 4-6-0 as pilot! On 21 September 1975, No 1306 *Mayflower* and No 4472 head northwards on the East Coast main line near Sessay with a Liverpool– Newcastle charter.
John E. Oxley

Below:
Many types of locomotive which never before – or rarely – ventured onto the Settle & Carlisle have acquitted themselves well on this formidable route. One such is Southern Railway 'Merchant Navy' Pacific No 35028 *Clan Line,* climbing between Kirkby Stephen and Birkett Tunnel with the southbound 'Lord Bishop' special on 30 September 1978.
J. H. Cooper-Smith

Above:
The York–Leeds–Harrogate–York circular tour is popular as a family day out. On 10 May 1980, this route saw the return of an LMS 'Duchess' Pacific to main line passenger work for the first time since the class was withdrawn from BR service late in 1964. No 46229 *Duchess of Hamilton* passes Headingley with one of the two 'Limited Edition' specials operated that day. *A. Bell*

Below:
When Great Western 'King' 4-6-0 No 6000 *King George V* ran regularly into Paddington, normal service speeds of 125mph were but a pipe dream. As the veteran marks the 125th anniversary of Paddington by heading a special to Didcot on 1 March 1979 there is more than a generation gap between it and the IC125 alongside. *B. W. Leslie*

A Decade of IC125s

Since their introduction, on the Western Region, towards the end of 1976, IC125s have extended their influence to the East Coast and Midland main lines and the northeast/southwest and southwest/northwest 'cross country' routes. Photographs on the next few pages show them in action nationwide.

Left:
A Class 253 IC125 heads westwards out of Bath across the River Avon on 22 September 1983.
Tim Perkins

Below left:
IC125s were introduced on services to and from St Pancras at the beginning of October 1982. A few

weeks earlier, on 20 August, a short formation passes through Kettering on a driver training trip.
Michael Ricks

Above:
The 11.00 from King's Cross is led into Edinburgh Waverley by power car No 43122 on 24 April 1982.
Mick Howarth

Below:
With power cars Nos 43175/76 – the latter billowing exhaust smoke – the 11.15 SO Newquay–Leeds approaches Bromsgrove on 3 July 1982, running some 25min late. The photographer reports that the IC125 managed to conquer Lickey Bank, which was just as well since bankers are not available on a Saturday afternoon. *Paul A. Biggs*

First application of the 'Executive' livery with which InterCity was relaunched in October 1983. Posing for photographic purposes on the Copy Pit line, power car No 43151 of unit No 253.028 wears the original variation, with the lighter colours continued across louvres on the bodyside and roof. *British Rail*

Above:
The first IC125 to visit the Southern Region was No 253.026, forming the 06.50 Plymouth–Paddington on 12 October 1980. The service was diverted from Exeter via Yeovil and Salisbury to Westbury because of engineering work and is seen during reversal at Salisbury. *G. F. Gillham*

Below:
Class 46 No 46.028 tows No 253.018, forming the 08.10 Newcastle–Plymouth, at Matford, near Exeter, on 1 May 1984. This was the Class 46's last duty before its withdrawal! *Peter Medley*

Above:
The original 'Executive' colour scheme proved impractical for obvious reasons and dark grey was extended over the louvres. Heading the first ECML set in the new livery, No 43085 *City of Bradford* stands at Stevenage on the 08.00 King's Cross–Aberdeen 'Aberdonian' on 15 March 1985.
David Percival

Below:
'We set off in that direction!' the pilotman seems to be telling the driver of No 43110 as the down 'Aberdonian' leaves Carlisle, diverted due to blockage of the ECML on 26 April 1980. *G. S. Cutts*

IC125 No 253.017 west of Bedwyn on 28 August 1979 working the down 'Cornish Riviera'. *M. Pope*

Preservation from the Falklands Conflict?

A. R. Robinson

While serving in the Falklands I was intrigued to see the remains of a narrow gauge War Department railway. Little information as to the origin and operation of this line seems to have survived over the years but the recent conflict has rekindled interest which may result in its preservation. A local historian, John Smith has some original photographs, of which the accompanying pictures are copies, and is keen to learn more of the Falklands' only railway.

It seems that the line was built before the turn of the century by the War Department and ran some 3½-4 miles from the military jetty at what is now called Navy Point to Moody Brook. The track was laid on level ground on the north side of the harbour, starting opposite the town of Port Stanley, and followed the shore to Moody Brook at the western end, the site of the Marine barracks. Alongside the barracks was a naval wireless station which generated its own electricity by means of steam turbines fed by coal-fired boilers. All the coal had to be brought in by sea and the railway was built for this purpose. There is also evidence that the railway conveyed ammunition and other military stores, as surfaced roads in the islands were few.

The track was laid to a gauge of 2ft 3in and was of light construction, using chairs spiked to wooden sleepers. These sleepers can still be seen along the whole length of the route and form the basis of a roadway. The jetty at the eastern end of the line was also a storage area and had a number of sidings and sheds where some of the wagon turntables and points remain. Today, the jetty is rotting and dangerous but the stone breakwaters are still sound and are used to moor small ships. At the end of the jetty is a scrap heap containing the jetty crane, large numbers of oil drums, thousands of beer cans and the remains of the two steam locomotives which worked the line. From these remains and the photographs we can see they were 0-4-0STs with open cabs, later boarded in. Few of the working parts and no manufacturer's plates remain on the locomotives which, at present, are little more than rusty scrap. The rolling stock seems to have been four-wheeled 'tippler' wagons plus the usual open

and flat wagons. Some underframes are on the scrap heap while others are dumped behind the storage sheds.

The railway also featured a unique form of locomotion which is well remembered locally. A sail-powered wagon, illustrated under the control of a lady driver, was used to travel back on the prevailing wind from Moody Brook to the harbour. Apparently, while popular with the staff, the idea was not so popular with the farmers over whose land the railway passed. The strong wind in the Falklands took the wagon to a good speed, but the braking for gates across the tracks left something to be desired!

As to the future, the railway has generated a great deal of interest amongst all levels of the Services in the Falklands. In particular, some of the engineering expertise now being put to developing the islands may become available for spare time projects. It is hoped that, with this help, at least one of the locomotives could be restored to static exhibition standards. However, before this can proceed premises must be found and these are in short supply; but with Service help a start will soon be made to preserve this small piece of Falklands heritage.

Top right:
One of the 0-4-0STs at the jetty with examples of rolling stock. *A. R. Robinson collection*

Far right, top:
A later photograph of one of the locomotives, with the boarded cab offering only slight relief from the prevailing winds! The locomotive is facing Moody Brook and the outskirts of Port Stanley can be seen on the opposite side of the harbour.
A. R. Robinson collection

Centre and bottom right:
The remains of a locomotive at Navy Point in late 1982. *A. R. Robinson*

Far right, bottom:
The braking system of the sail-powered wagon was rather less than effective but the 'bufferbeam' looks sturdy enough! *A. R. Robinson collection*

Pullmans on Tour

In addition to their use on the 'Venice Simplon Orient Express', the Pullman Cars which form, arguably, the most magnificent rake of coaching stock seen for many years travel far and wide on charter work, hauled by a variety of locomotive types.

Left:
Class 45 No 45.141 heads the train southwards at Wigston South Junction on a Nottingham–London charter working on 21 April 1984. The second vehicle, an LNER brake now Baggage Car No 7, is well-matched but Baggage Car No 9 (formerly a BR corridor brake second) is perhaps slightly out of place. *R. M. Rixon*

Above left:
A startling combination of liveries on 17 June 1984 as '73' No 73.123 *Gatwick Express* heads the 11.44 Victoria–Folkestone Harbour 'Venice Simplon Orient Express' past Petts Wood Junction. The locomotive and train also represent contrasting eras of international travel. *David Brown*

Above:
In charge of a Waterloo–Brockenhurst excursion on 7 May 1983 is Class 33 No 33.056 *The Burma Star*. *David J. Kimber*

Above:
The Burma Star is seen again with the Pullmans, passing the site of Breidden station (closed in September 1960) on the Shrewsbury–Welshpool line on 6 July 1984. The charter from London Victoria, by the Development Board for Rural Wales, brought a Class 33 to Newtown for the first time, it is believed.
Andrew Bannister

Below:
Photographed appropriately near Cockshute, Stoke-on-Trent, the Pullmans are headed by Class 86 No 86.206 *City of Stoke-on-Trent* on 21 March 1984.
C. J. Tuffs

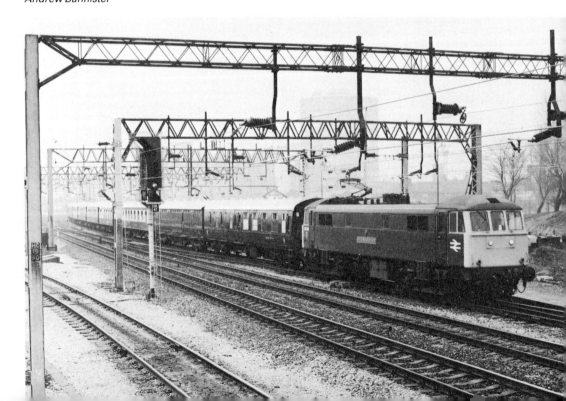

Above:
Prepared at short notice for a King's Cross–
Harrogate 'Fashion Fair' charter on 14 March 1983,
Class 47 No 47.415's appearance did not match the
pristine Pullmans. The train is passing Wymondley,
between Stevenage and Hitchin. *David Percival*

Below:
The 'Wine Fair Special' from London Victoria on 12
July 1984 leaves Bristol Temple Meads behind '37' No
37.206 on the last lap of its journey to Wapping
Wharf. Class 37 No 37.229 *The Cardiff Rod Mill* is
attached at the rear in preparation for the return trip.
Geoff Cann

A Quartet of Tanks

Above:
**GWR '4200' 2-8-0T No 5239 *Goliath* storms through
Goodrington Sands Halt on the Torbay & Dartmouth
Railway with a train for Kingswear in May 1983.**
J. Stocker

Left:
**A quiet moment for LMS '3F' 0-6-0T No 16440 and
crew on 27 June 1982 before departure from
Butterley, Midland Railway Trust.**   *Bob Avery*

Above right:
**Returned to its former stamping ground, Southern
Railway Class A1X 0-6-0T No 8 *Freshwater* heads an
Isle of Wight Steam Railway train at Woodhouse
Farm on 6 September 1981.**   *M. Pope*

Right:
**With its destination board correctly in place, LNER
'N2' 0-6-2T No 4744 departs from Loughborough, on
the Great Central Railway, with the 10.00 to Rothley
on 13 May 1980.**   *W. A. Sharman*

The Railways of South Humberside

Martin Bairstow

The County of Humberside was a product of the 1972 Local Government Act, created, one suspects, primarily as a declaration of faith in the eventual completion of the Humber road bridge. Until the opening of this structure in 1981 the only link between the two parts of Humberside was a railway-owned paddle steamer. A proper railway connection across the Humber never came remotely near to being achieved – not even in the days when railway engineers were successfully overcoming the natural barriers of the Forth, the Tay and the Severn. These other estuaries lay across the paths of main lines but the inconvenience of crossing the Humber by ferry affected only local traffic. Both sides enjoyed separate main line facilities and a railway bridge never seemed urgent.

Today, South Humberside is the one area where the network of the former Great Central Railway remains substantially intact. The principal town is Grimsby which, together with the neighbouring resort of Cleethorpes, is served by InterCity trains to Manchester via Doncaster and Sheffield and to Kings Cross via Lincoln and Newark. Local diesel multiple-units also leave Cleethorpes by these two routes whilst there are three trains per day to Sheffield via Gainsborough and Retford. All three routes are combined between Cleethorpes and Barnetby.

As far as Habrough, the main line also carries an hourly DMU from Cleethorpes to Barton-on-Humber. This was a new service introduced in 1981.

Below:
The 13.00 Cleethorpes–King's Cross IC125 passes a reminder of earlier days near Market Rasen on 15 July 1984. *B. J. Beer*

Prior to that date, the branch north of Habrough had seen a rather less frequent service running to New Holland Pier in connection with the Humber ferry, and Barton had been a branch off a branch, with a train just running 3½ miles from New Holland. It was only the physical difficulty of getting buses up the pier to the ferry landing stage which had allowed both these branches to survive two formal closure proposals during the 1960s. Yet when the *raison d'etre* for these trains was taken away on withdrawal of the ferry, the service was not only retained but improved.

This article sets out to consider the history and present prospects of the line from Cleethorpes to Barton-on-Humber. In addition, it features the port of Immingham which was established by the GCR to rival Grimsby and which has succeeded in outgrowing its older neighbour. Immingham generates a good deal of railway freight traffic but no longer sees any passenger trains.

Powers to bring railways into South Humberside were given to the Great Grimsby & Sheffield Junction Railway in June 1845. A main line was to be built from Grimsby to Gainsborough with branches to Market Rasen and to New Holland. By the end of 1845 the company had amalgamated with the Sheffield & Lincolnshire Junction and with the Sheffield, Ashton & Manchester Railways to form the Manchester, Sheffield & Lincolnshire Railway. An Act of June 1846 authorised the extension of the Market Rasen line to Lincoln together with a branch from New Holland to Barton-on-Humber.

The Railway's interest in New Holland lay in its proximity to Hull. Ferries had operated across the Humber since medieval times and had employed steam power since 1814. In January 1845, various members of the provisional committee of the Great Grimsby & Sheffield Junction Railway, the future directors of the company, purchased the ferries for £10,000 then, nine months later, resold them to the Railway for £21,000. They used their privileged position to secure a personal profit of about £500,000 in today's currency and, although the matter was brought to light by a committee of shareholders in 1850, they got away with it.

The first section of railway to be completed was from Grimsby to New Holland, opened on 1 March 1848. At New Holland the line ran along a pier some 500yd in length with continuous platforms each side. At the near end these constituted New Holland Town station and at the far end New Holland Pier where passengers and freight transferred to the ferry for Hull. Further openings took place on 1 November 1848 from Ulceby to Brigg and from Barnetby to Market Rasen. The extension to Lincoln followed on 18 December and the single track branch from New Holland to Barton-on-Humber opened on 1 March 1849.

Above:
A Cleethorpes—Barton on Humber train accelerates away from Barrow Haven, the only intermediate station between New Holland and Barton, on 9 April 1983. *Martin Bairstow*

With the inauguration of the Brigg-Gainsborough section on 2 April 1849 the Great Grimsby & Sheffield Junction Railway was complete. It only remained to close the gap between Sheffield and Gainsborough on 16 July 1849 to achieve a continuous railway from Manchester.

Below:
Class 47 No 47.222 powers through Barnetby with coal from Thoresby in the Nottinghamshire coalfield bound for Immingham. *Clive Jarrad*

New Holland Pier on 5 April 1980, some 14 months before the opening of the Humber Bridge; the left hand platform was the 'road' to the ferry. A Class 114 DMU waits to form the 15.11 to Cleethorpes.
Les Bertram

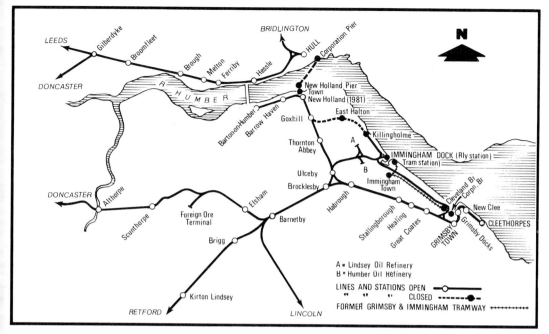

A single line opened from Grimsby to Cleethorpes on 6 April 1863. This was doubled by 1874 and began to carry a very heavy passenger traffic during the 1880s when the Manchester, Sheffield & Lincolnshire Railway embarked upon the commercial development of Cleethorpes as a holiday resort.

The final stage in main line railway construction in South Humberside came with the opening in 1866 of the Trent, Ancholme & Grimsby Railway (a part of the MS&LR) which completed the route from Doncaster via Scunthorpe to Barnetby.

The first train service from Grimsby to New Holland offered five return workings, with two on Sundays. When services began operating through from Manchester there were five weekday trains from Manchester to New Holland with connctions there for Hull and at Ulceby for Grimsby.

The 1880 timetable still showed five weekday trains between Manchester and New Holland and two on Sundays confirming that the MS&LR still regarded New Holland as being the terminus of its main line to Hull, with Grimsby and Cleethorpes just a branch. There were seven weekday trains direct from New Holland to Cleethorpes and three on Sundays but there were also connections available at Brocklesby for passengers wishing to complete this journey. The New Holland-Barton branch carried 14 weekday trains plus an extra one on Thursdays only and four on Sundays. All stopped by request at Barrow Haven and most had connections to and from Hull.

After 1888 main line trains from Manchester and Sheffield operated to Cleethorpes, leaving New Holland passengers to change at Brocklesby station which was suitably enlarged with two island platforms. The 1910 timetable showed nine weekday departures from New Holland to Brocklesby with two extras on Thursdays. There were six through trains to Cleethorpes which could also be reached by some of the Brocklesby services. The Barton service was of the same pattern as that of 30 years earlier, except that Barrow Haven had become a compulsory stop. All train departures from New Holland had advertised connections from Hull although many gave passengers waits of over 30min at New Holland. This was in contrast to the arrangements for the former through Manchester trains where the advertised departures from Hull were consistently 30min in advance of

Left:

Grimsby Docks on 2 September 1974, with a Class 114 unit departing on the 12.57 New Holland–Cleethorpes service. *B. G. Barrett*

those from New Holland, allowing just 10min to effect the change.

Through LNER days and into the BR period little changed at New Holland. *Bradshaw* for 1957 showed a dozen departures on both the Barton and Cleethorpes lines but with no trains to Brocklesby. Passengers travelling towards Sheffield or Doncaster now had to change at Habrough.

The line from Habrough to New Holland, together with the Barton branch, was threatened with closure during the 1960s but both were reprieved in 1969 thanks mainly to the difficulty of serving the ferries by road. The ferry service had been 'modernised' in 1934 with the construction of floating landing stages at each terminus to provide 'roll on – roll off' facilities for motor cars and commercial vehicles. These had to drive along the platform flanking the tracks on New Holland Pier to reach the *Wingfield Castle* or *Tattersal Castle* – two new paddle steamers introduced in 1934. These vessels were joined by the *Lincoln Castle* in 1940 and each gave almost 40 years' service.

The 1880s had seen an unsuccessful bill for a railway from Hull to Lincoln using a Humber bridge. There had followed trial borings sponsored by the MS&LR for a Humber tunnel but moves to get trains across the river progressed no further. By the 1960s the fashion was to build road bridges across major estuaries and the Government authorised plans to bridge the Humber. Long before this work was actually started, talk of a bridge had imposed a planning blight on the Humber ferries and associated rail services. The ex-Southern Railway diesel paddle vessel *Farringford* was 'imported' to continue the Humber ferry in 1974, after the two older paddle steamers had been withdrawn, and maintained the service single handed after the withdrawal of the *Lincoln Castle* in 1978.

The ferry was not popular. Motorists regarded it as a nuisance and looked forward to the opening of the bridge. Rail/ferry passengers had little to lose from the threatened withdrawal of both the ferry and associated rail services since most journeys, especially from Barton, would be faster and cheaper once they could travel by bus or by car across the bridge.

In the final years the *Farringford* was crossing the Humber 10 times daily except when 'circumstances outside the Board's control' intervened in the form of low tides – sometimes as often as twice a day. Most sailings still had train connections to both Cleethorpes and Barton, though not to Barton on Sundays. It seemed inevitable that trains would cease with the ferry.

However, we were now in an era when rail closures were no longer as popular as in the 1960s and BR was saved the unpalatable task of proposing closure of the New Holland lines when Humberside County Council announced its plans for public transport following completion of the bridge. An hourly train service, roughly double the previous frequency, was to operate between Cleethorpes and Barton, calling at a resited station at New Holland so as to avoid reversal. Connection was to be made at Barton station with an hourly Scunthorpe-Hull bus service. The County Council claimed that the Hull-Cleethorpes journey time would be shorter by this method than by bus throughout. This is questionable, in that a through bus going straight from Barton to Grimsby might have been quicker but would have left the railway with only the intermediate traffic or alternatively would have left New Holland and the other intermediate villages without a service had the railway closed. BR negotiated a deal with the County Council involving a measure of revenue support and contribution to capital cost of the alterations. The amount involved is negligible compared to the price BR would have had to charge in a PTE area. As Humberside is a shire county, BR could take into account the need to retain the line for freight and so offer the improved passenger service at marginal cost.

The new service to Hull is faster than the former train and ferry from all points except possibly from New Holland itself. It has a further advantage in running to Paragon station which is better both for connecting trains and for the city centre than was the former Hull Corporation Pier 'station'. A limited range of through tickets is available, except from unstaffed stations, and facilities such as BR railcards are not valid for the bus part of the journey. If the Barton-Hull bus could be advertised as part of the BR network with full ticketing facilities – for example, if a Cleethorpes-Scarborough fare were valid that way with Persil tickets, railcards, etc – then its value might be enhanced. As it is, the predominant use of the

Left:
The level crossing gates between the staggered platforms at Habrough have just closed behind a 'Trans-Pennine' unit, pausing on a Manchester Piccadilly–Cleethorpes service on 9 April 1983. Manchester–Humberside services have been locomotive-hauled since May 1984. *Martin Bairstow*

Above:
Class 47 No 47.412 awaits departure from Cleethorpes with the 17.37 to King's Cross on 29 June 1977 as a Class 114 DMU arrives on a service from Sheffield. *Stanley Creer*

service is restricted to journeys within South Humberside and only a small amount of traffic is using the Barton 'interchange' for its intended purpose. Most of the former rail/ferry passengers are presumably travelling by car.

The train service has been slightly reduced with the loss of two evening trains. It is probable that the Ulceby-New Holland section may be reduced to single track but that will not affect the service. It would need several separate bus services to serve the intermediate villages and with a flow of chemicals by rail from Barton to Corkicle (near Whitehaven) the future seems reasonably secure.

BR now threatens to reduce the Cleethorpes-Barton on Humber service from 14 to nine trains each way. The reason given for this is the granting of a licence for a through Cleethorpes-Hull bus service. In the absence of proper marketing and

ticketing to Hull, and with the 23-mile train journey alone taking 57 minutes, this can hardly come as a surprise. Meanwhile, a new source of rail freight has been established with the opening of grain loading facilities on the site of the former New Holland Town station.

One of the constituents of the MS&LR was the Grimsby Docks Co which had been incorporated as the Grimsby Haven Co in 1796 and opened the Grimsby Old Dock in 1801. Under railway ownership the port facilities were expanded during the 19th century to include the Royal and Alexander Docks and three fish docks.

In 1874 the MS&LR was advised that a dock in the Immingham/Killingholme area would have navigational advantages over Grimsby but no action was taken until the passing of the Humber Commercial Railway & Dock Act in 1904. Work on the construction of Immingham Dock began in 1906 and it was opened on 22 July 1912 when King George V sailed in aboard the Hull-New Holland paddle steamer *Killingholme*.

Immingham was connected to the rest of the Great Central system by three railways plus an electric tramway. The first of these to open, in 1906, was the Grimsby District Light Railway running from West Marsh Junction to Immingham. Initially it was used by the contractors but on 3 January 1910 a steam railcar began running four times a day between temporary halts at Pyewipe Road, on the edge of Grimsby, and at Immingham.

Meanwhile work had begun on laying a parallel electric tramway. This began at Corporation Bridge, Grimsby, and ran through the street to Cleveland Bridge, then alongside the steam

Left:
The Humber ferry, paddle steamer *Lincoln Castle,* at New Holland Pier on 16 March 1974. *Martin Bairstow*

operated line but without any physical connection. Both lines were single track with passing loops. The electric service opened from Corporation Bridge to Immingham Town on 15 May 1912, whereupon the steam service ceased. The 5½-mile electric line offered a frequent passenger service. On 17 November a 1½-mile double track extension was opened to the eastern jetty of Immingham Dock. Trams had to reverse at Immingham Town. A further short branch of the tramway was completed in 1915 between Immingham Town and Queens Road to serve Immingham Village but was never brought into use.

It was intended to connect the tramway with the Great Grimsby Street Tramways Company which operated services within the town and to Cleethorpes. The GCR would then have exercised running powers to Grimsby Town Station but this entailed strengthening the Corporation Bridge across the old Dock to carry trams. This was done in 1928 but the Grimsby trams were then in decline and the connection was never built.

Proposals by BR to close the Grimsby & Immingham tramway were initially rejected by the TUCC but from 1 July 1956 the street section in Grimsby was closed and for the next five years the service started from Cleveland Bridge. Then, although the distance by road was nearly double that by rail, the line closed completely on 30 June 1961.

The 'main line' to Immingham, at least for freight, runs from Ulceby to Immingham Dock where the station was on the western jetty separated by the dock entrance from the electric

Above:
Buses running in both directions on the Hull–Scunthorpe service make the rail connection at Barton on Humber on 9 April 1983. *Martin Bairstow*

tramway station. This, the Humber Commercial Railway, carried its first consignment of coal on 29 June 1910 and was completed in 1912 to a total route mileage of 8¼ which includes the connection with the Grimsby District Light Railway around the perimeter of the docks. The line did not carry passenger trains until a rush hour working from Grimsby via Ulceby was introduced on closure of the tramway. This then lasted until October 1969.

The final railway connection to Immingham was the Barton & Immingham Light Railway which opened from a junction with the New Holland-Habrough line at Goxhill in 1911. A passenger service operated from New Holland Pier to Immingham Dock until June 1963. The 1938 timetable shows six Mondays to Fridays trains with two extra on Saturdays, but no Sunday service. By 1960 when DMUS were in operation there was one train less each day. This branch was closed completely north of Killingholme in June 1963.

Right:
Car No 14 of the Grimsby & Immingham tramway stands at Corporation Bridge station, Grimsby, on 25 September 1955. *J. C. W. Halliday*

Meanwhile the Immingham complex provides BR with a considerable volume of freight traffic. This is in total contrast to the neighbouring ports of Grimsby and Hull, where a complete withdrawal of rail freight facilities has been discussed though not actually carried out. Immingham witnesses both the import and export of coal. Imported iron ore is transported in rotary tipplers from Immingham to Santon Foreign Ore Terminal which is situated on a short branch east of Scunthorpe. Steel is another commodity which is both imported and exported. This apparently illogical traffic can be created by 'dumping' – that is selling abroad at below market price so as to keep up both production levels and the domestic price. The exercise is a bit futile if overseas manufacturers are doing the same. Nevertheless in 1979 a Section 8 grant of £574,000 was approved towards the provision of facilities to service substantial tonnages of this traffic for rail haulage.

The Humber and Lindsey oil refineries are served by short branches off the Humber Commercial Railway and from here oil is carried by rail to most parts of the North of England. The Grimsby District Light Railway serves chemical works at Courtaulds, British Titan Products and Ciba-Geigy, and there is a Fisons Fertilizer plant just south of Immingham.

Below:
Except during the 1960s, the Humber Commercial Railway line between Ulceby and Immingham Dock has always been a freight-only route; its traffic includes oil trains from the Lindsey and Humber refineries. On 30 June 1977, Class 47 No 47.219 draws a train off the branch at Ulceby and joins the line from New Holland. *Stanley Creer*

Bottom:
Two Class 37s stand at the head of a 2,100 ton iron ore train under the loading bunkers at Immingham in August 1974. *Colin Boocock*

'08s' in the Limelight

Those unsung stalwarts of freight yards, carriage sidings and station environs, the Class 08 shunters occasionally have their moments when they travel more than just a few yards before changing direction as these six photographs show.

Right:
An '08' on a 'proper' train – complete with brake van! On 23 July 1984, No 08.033 passes Rotherham Road with a trip freight to BSC Parkgate. *Keith Hacker*

Below:
On the main line. At Ipswich on 5 August 1984, No 08.752 heads the wiring train during completion of the final section of 'overhead' between Colchester and Ipswich Tunnel. *Ian Cowley*

Above:
A charming and unusual rural view of No 08.539 with a train of loaded coal wagons for the Earles cement factory in the Hope Valley, joining the branch from the main line on 23 November 1975. *L. A. Nixon*

Right:
No. 08.259 was the first member of class 08 to be reduced in height in order to work the Gwendraeth valley line between the opencast site at Cwmmawr and Coedbach washery, with its restricted loading gauge, replacing life-expired members of class 03. The work was carried out at Landore depot and the newly modified locomotive is seen on a test run on 16 July 1984.
British Rail

Above:
To the rescue of a Class 37! Assistance arrived in the shape of No 08.942 after '37' No 37.191 failed in the Bristol area while heading a coal train from Severn Tunnel Junction on 26 August 1981. Slow progress is made past Ashton Junction at the end of the shunter's moment of glory. *John Chalcraft*

Below:
The sound of an '08' and a couple of fully laden scrap metal wagons on the move is best left to the imagination! No 08.946 leaves Becket Street Goods, Oxford, on 10 August 1983 with a transfer working to Hinksey Yard. *C. J. M. Lofthus*

A Great Steam Show

George C. Dickinson

Even in 7¼in gauge the massive proportions of a Union Pacific 4-8-8-4 'Big Boy' cannot fail to impress, as demonstrated by No 4008 *William Jeffers* of the Forest Railroad Park. *Forest Railroad Park*

Among the world's greatest steam shows there was little to challenge the supremacy of North America, where the locomotives were in a class by themselves. In steam engine construction, if an idea was theoretically possible it was usually tried in practice. Rigid framed machines stretched out to 12 coupled wheels, Mallet-style semi-articulateds with 16 were built by the hundred, while one class of ten engines even had 20 coupled wheels. The ultimate manifestation, before all was swept away, was the Union Pacific Railroad's 4-8-8-4 'Big Boy', a 540ton giant which collected all the superlatives in the language – even the American language. Several of the 25 examples have been preserved but, up to 1984, none had run in America for over 20 years.

It might raise a few eyebrows to state that the first 'Big Boy' to steam since UP ceased using them did so in England in 1978, but that is indeed the case. This particular 'Big Boy' is a 7¼in gauge miniature. The railway on which it runs is a little off the general railfan's beaten track but, let no mistake be made, the Forest Railroad Park at Dobwalls, in Cornwall, is a first class enterprise all the way. Owned and operated by John Southern and his family, it is also unique in these islands.

First and foremost it is an all-American system, with two lines, each approaching a mile in length, paying unabashed tribute to the Union Pacific and Rio Grande Railroads and to the people who built and managed them. In 1983 there were six steam engines and three diesels, all of different types. The entire motive power fleet could be sampled by referring to the published roster and visiting Dobwalls on three suitable days, visits after the first being at a discount price. One ride is included in the admission charge and subsequent rides are reasonably priced.

Structures and features on each route are named after real places on the prototype roads (though

Chattanooga seems a bit misplaced!) and the names of the various passes and tunnels will be familiar to readers of American railroad literature. The UP line includes a genuine 1 in 64 Sherman Hill, with tunnels on the upgrade. These tunnels are an experience in themselves. My visit in 1983 coincided with a spell of legendary 'American weather' with a brilliant sun shining out of a clear blue sky. Entering the Aspen Tunnel the train passed from full sunlight into a gloomy acrid atmosphere pervaded by cloying warmth and dampness from swirling coal smoke and clinging steam. Seen through this haze of locomotive exhaust, the daylight ahead appeared a dark orange-brown, progressively brightening until, suddenly, the sun was blazing down again and there was refreshing cool air to breathe once more. The sequence was repeated a few moments later in the Hermosa Tunnel.

Lineside features include American water cranes, fed from wooden towers, scale telegraph poles, an attractive locomotive depot with turntable, a miniature Ames Monument atop Sherman Hill, bridges, forests, rock-sided cuttings and other scenic artefacts. Even though the track is fully fenced for safety, there are a number of good locations for train watching and some suitable for photography. The locomotive shed and workshop has a viewing walkway along its full length but, on fine days, most of the resting engines are displayed outside on the turntable fan. The visual features are audibly complemented by regular sequences of locomotive exhaust sounds and American whistles.

Above the carriage shed is an exhibition hall in which each railroad is portrayed in photographs and in a 50ft diorama. The UP display includes a pair of 'Big Boys' toiling to Sherman Summit, trailing a massive freight; recorded descriptions of the scene are available alongside. At the end of the hall is a continuous video presentation about the two railroads and the Forest Park system, changed on a three-day rota. A separate covered area is devoted to a photographic history of the Forest Park project and nearby is a gallery housing a large and important collection of Archibald Thorburn's famous wildlife and bird paintings, thoughtfully provided for those who can tear themselves away from the steam trains!

The park is in open rural surroundings and offers distant views from Sherman Hill. Pleasant walkways thread the site, crossing the railway tracks and linking the various buildings with the picnic places and children's play areas. In the field

Left:
The wooden water-tower and pines add a touch of authenticity at Dobwalls station, where Union Pacific 4-8-4 No 818 *Queen of Wyoming* stands ready to depart on 18 July 1978. *Brian Morrison*

of catering, the establishment sets a standard for others to emulate. The main cafe is in the station building, overlooking the running lines. Its interior is rather like a very wide dining car; the decor is polished wood and the walls carry paintings of American railroad scenes by Paul Gribble. The whole operation bears the impress of personal care and enthusiastic management.

No doubt there are people who will protest that Forest Park is *only* a 7¼in gauge miniature railway and therefore not worth a serious enthusiast's time and effort to visit. Such people presumably never have time for model railways either! What, then, does Forest Park provide for the discerning enthusiast? It offers an experience of a reasonably authentic American Railroad using coal-fired steam engines, accessible to the public without travelling abroad. It operates the largest 4-8-4s working in the British Isles, as well as the first working 'Big Boy'. This latter machine gives a practical demonstration of the working of a big Mallet locomotive, with the opportunity to see a double set of eight-coupled wheels running together and to observe the effect of 'throw over' on curves. The looped track enables each train to be viewed several times and from different angles, with a minimum of walking, while the frequent service allows any particular scene to be observed many times. With the acceptance that a miniature cannot truly replace the full-sized prototype, and that a fair measure of imagination must be exercised, three points must not be overlooked. First, although D&RGW 3ft gauge 2-8-2s do still run in the USA, they are themselves on 'preserved' railways. Second, the UP system – indeed the whole USA main line network – is steamless but for the very occasional special workings by preserved locomotives. Third, full-size standard gauge steam railways in this country are preservation operations which also require a degree of imagination to bridge the gap to authenticity, even in the context of main line running.

It must, therefore, be concluded that the best of the public miniature railways have much to offer and that the enthusiast who excludes them from his interests is denying himself a great deal of genuine pleasure. If he omits the Forest Railroad Park his loss is indeed considerable.

Below:
A well-loaded train on 18 July 1978 is headed by 2-8-2 No 488 *General Palmer*, a 7¼in gauge version of a Rio Grande original. *Brian Morrison*

Nostalgia for Nine Elms

During the mid-1960s I eagerly looked forward to any organised tour of London locomotive depots which included Nine Elms. Maybe the depot lacked a wide variety of locomotive types, particularly in the later years, but the photographic possibilities were almost limitless. Every visit provided new angles and lighting effects. Even today, when I look out from the Waterloo train passing Nine Elms, the sight of Covent Garden market fades and my mind's eye sees vivid images of 20 years ago.

Below:
Steam from Standard '3' 2-6-2T No 82026 disperses amidst the roof structure on 24 January 1965. The delicate pattern contrasts with the unmistakable bulk of an unrebuilt 'light' Pacific – 'Battle of Britain' No 34051 *Winston Churchill*. The date is significant, for Sir Winston Churchill died that very day; six days later, his funeral train was hauled by the Pacific which bore his name. *David Percival*

Above:
Its career on Waterloo empty stock workings ending a few weeks earlier, withdrawn Class E4 0-6-2T No 32487 stands in the yard on 27 January 1963 with a 'Q1' 0-6-0 alongside. *David Percival*

Right:
A batch of Standard '3' 2-6-2Ts was drafted in for ECS duties at the end of 1962. No 82016 rests just inside the shed on 19 January 1963 with withdrawn 'Schools' 4-4-0s Nos 30903 *Charterhouse* and 30935 *Sevenoaks* in the background. *David Percival*

Below:
One of the more unusual types to appear before my camera at Nine Elms, Class Q 0-6-0 No 30530 is seen in company with Standard '5' 4-6-0 No 73112 *Morgan Le Fay* on 24 January 1965. *David Percival*

Aspects of shed work at Nine Elms

Above:
Framed by railings, Standard '5' No 73110 *The Red Knight* has its fire raked out over the ash pit on 29 January 1966. The grab-crane used for loading ash wagons has a decrepit appearance, signalling the approaching end of steam. *David Percival*

Below:
The fireman keeps a careful watch as unrebuilt 'West Country' Pacific No 34102 *Lapford* rolls onto the turntable on 14 January 1967. *David Percival*

Above right:
Tube-cleaning on another unrebuilt 'West Country' – No 34002 *Salisbury* on 11 December 1966. Standard '3' 2-6-2T No 82029 waits its turn. *David Percival*

Below right:
'Merchant Navy' 4-6-2 No 35027 *Port Line* joins three 'light' Pacifics at the coaling plant on 30 January 1965. Ahead of it in the queue are Nos 34009 *Lyme Regis,* 34056 *Croydon* and 34093 *Saunton.*
David Percival

Left:
After the rebuilding of 'Battle of Britain' No 34090 *Sir Eustace Missenden, Southern Railway*, its massive nameplate seemed somewhat incongruously perched on the running plate. The Pacific, minus its tender, is in the repair bay at Nine Elms on 30 January 1965. *David Percival*

Below left:
One of the depot's Standard '4' 4-6-0s, No 75076 shows its double chimney in silhouette on 14 January 1967. *David Percival*

Above:
Standards and Pacifics – a typical collection of motive power in the final years. On 14 January 1967 the winter sun picks out 'West Country' No 34032

Camelford,* whose nameplates and smokebox numberplate have been removed. Also visible are Standard '5' 4-6-0s Nos 73029 and 73115 *King Pellinore,* Standard '4' 2-6-4T No 80089 and the tender of 'Merchant Navy' No 35013 *Blue Funnel. *David Percival*

Below:
A final memory – the evening of 2 June 1967, just five weeks before closure, finds Nine Elms already showing signs of neglect. The grab of the ash-disposal crane has no work, weeds gain hold in the once-hostile ground and 'West Country' No 34021 *Dartmoor,* clean but without nameplates, is the only arrival. A Standard '3' 2-6-2T bustles past with empty stock for Clapham Junction but the weary gait of the solitary fitter tells it all. *David Percival*

The Breakneck and Murder

M. C. Batten

The mid-1950s was the high water mark for the railway system in South Wales, at least since the Great War. Apart from such byways as Cowbridge-Aberthaw and one or two lines in the valleys, the system remained largely intact. Dozens of pits were still working and, although the volume of coal traffic could not be compared with the boom years, it was substantial. An afternoon in any of the valleys soon dispelled the suspicion that all those relief lines were a luxury. The changes wrought in the years since have left little clue to the younger enthusiast – or, indeed, railway employee – as to the endless procession of trains that we thought of as normal.

To the outsider, South Wales is usually thought of as a grubby expanse of old waste tips and derelict industries. This is true to some extent but it is only a small part of the overall environment and it used to be possible to spend a day travelling by train through beautiful and often spectacular scenery. An easy way for me to 'get away from it all' was a trip on the Brecon&Merthyr, that most delightful of railways. It was always an adventure and, for the first timer, the names of its stations were an unvisited music: Pontsticill, Dolygaer, Torpantau, Pentir Rhiw, Talybont-on-Usk and Talyllyn Junction.

To begin at the beginning, a typical day would find me on the platform at Cadoxton waiting for the 2pm Barry Island-Merthyr. On one such day it arrives behind Standard 2-6-2T No 82029 in the capable hands of driver 'Rolly' Marsh. Now Rolly was one of that rare breed of enginemen who believed in getting from A to B in the shortest possible time. He also enjoyed company on the footplate and as the train grinds to a halt he shouts down from the side window: 'Dinas Powis!' The remainder of the journey then becomes one of dodging higher authority. Onto the footplate at Dinas Powis, off again at Grangetown; on again at Llandaff, off again at Treforest; on again at Abercynon and off, finally, at Pentrebach. Those Class 3 tanks must have been the roughest ever to disgrace the South Wales railways. People wrote letters to the *South Wales Echo* complaining about the disturbance as they slipped violently attempting to restart trains at Dingle Road Halt on Penarth Bank. The cabs were generously proportioned and well appointed, with an upholstered seat for the driver, but to actually sit there with the locomotive working could be a shattering experience. It was something akin to bare back riding, only harder. One driver, who shall remain nameless, attempted to obtain compensation for cracked dentures on the grounds of driving an '82'. Actually he fell over after a particularly heavy session in the 'Snivs'!*

To come back to Rolly Marsh, he was a man in the Bill Hoole mould and I often wondered what would have happened if he'd been let loose on the main line. He was known in the trade as a 'big handle man', meaning that he was very fond of the regulator. He believed there were only two positions for that particular control – wide open or slammed shut. The noise and vibration of that trip to Merthyr lives with me now. The blessed relief of waiting time at just about every stop followed by the merciless thrashing in a permanent haze of dancing coal dust; the fireman sweating like a pig and the searing heat from the backplate. I tried my hand at firing the thing, but only succeeded in bending the lip of the shovel and throwing coal all over Rolly's feet. All this went on to the accompaniment of a continuous stream of invective from the driver's seat. It was 'a poor tool'; it would 'lose its feet in the Sahara'; you could 'give me a Taff "A" any time'; whoever designed it 'wanted to come and drive it' and so on. The pause at Abercynon was notable for the argument with Bill Hughes, the guard, over the state of his journal and how he couldn't send it in with all this time gained. Rolly looked down his considerable nose at Bill. 'You worries too much Bill. You want to make it out *after* the journey, like everybody else.' Bill, immaculate as ever, with fresh buttonhole, went off in a huff, much to the amusement of the crew of the 3.25pm to Aberdare (Low Level). What a splendid sight *that* train was with two post nationalisation auto-coaches and a

*The 'Snivs' was the name of the local BR Staff Association club. Origin unknown.

Above:
Standard '3' 2-6-2T No 82041 approaches Dinas Powis on 1 September 1955 with the 10am Barry Island-Merthyr. *S. Rickard*

'6400' Pannier in spotless lined green. And so to Pentrebach, where I left the footplate. An army of ticket collectors checked the whole train; Merthyr was undergoing some alterations at the time which rendered it temporarily 'open'. All this caused considerable delay which gave Rolly the chance of a final fling. We rolled into Merthyr at precisely 3.43pm, one minute early. It took a much needed wash in the porters' room before I felt fit to face the world and the 4.15pm to Pontsticill Junction.

From here the journey would become a transport of delight. The auto-train pulls out of the dead end of Merthyr behind a '5500' and we bustle gently over Mardy Junction on to the GWR line to Hirwaun. We leave it again, almost immediately, at Rhydycar where we branch right onto the Brecon & Merthyr and London & North Western Joint line. Anyone who thinks the Festiniog was the first to have a spiral in these islands should think again, for this railway was precisely that, on a grand scale with spectacular engineering works. Working hard against the grade, the '5500' keeps working until the last possible moment before coming to a halt at Heolgerrig. On then to Cefn Coed and its

spectacular stone viaduct. Even Cyfarthfa Castle, fortified home of the notorious ironmaster Crawshay Bailey, pales into insignificance beneath this fine structure. Next to Pontsarn for Vaynor, where the guard lights the solitary oil lamp at the unstaffed halt. The fact that the 'f' is missing from the word 'for' on the signboard gives the place an air of uncertainty and, still wondering precisely where we are, we move off to Morlais Junction and the end of the joint line. Here a trainload of schoolchildren is waiting, just outside the tunnel. The pannier tank at its head is blowing off noisily and partly obscuring the LMS signal with steam.

We're on to B&M metals proper, now, and soon we can see the embankment carrying the B&M main line above us at 1 to the right. We come alongside it at the island platform of Pontsticill Junction. This station was always a joy to behold with a well kept garden sloping down from the stationmaster's house to the down platform. I may be wrong, but I believe this house was a farmhouse, built long before the railway and subsequently incorporated into the station. The air is fresh and a cool breeze snipes off the surface of the Taf Fechan Reservoir. Fish are rising and snapping at flies and away in the distance the distinctive bark of an Ivatt Class 2 can be heard approaching with the 3pm Newport (High Street)-Brecon. The 2-6-0, No

Above:
At Merthyr on 8 January 1960, '6400' 0-6-0PT No 6436 simmers vigorously at the head of the 3.18pm auto train to Hirwaun. *R. T. M. Hoyle*

46512, now the property of the Strathspey Railway, fusses in. It should feel at home in the Highlands. The four coach train consists of Collett corridor brake composite, Collett corridor third, Stanier corridor third and Collett brake third. Although it is high summer, it is good to get into the warmth of the train and we are off on the climb to Dolygaer where we pause to conform with the timetable. In years past the little station had played host to thousands who visited the area for regattas on the reservoirs but not a living soul moves today. A brief flutter of green from the guard's window and we continue the climb to Torpantau where we pause for water and token exchange. Here, 1,300ft above sea level, the railway looks at home with its lack of clutter and low strong buildings to keep out the severe winters. Two little girls climb down and go to the water column with a bowl for their black and white collie dog. The fireman obliges and the dog's tail wags happily at the scent of refreshment.

With all these formalities completed we resume climbing and plunge into the dark bore of Torpantau Tunnel. Almost immediately, the gradient eases and we pick up speed as we begin to descend. This is the highest tunnel above sea level in the British Isles and as if to underline the fact we burst out into spectacular scenery of ancient mountains and man made lakes far below. We continue to accelerate as we dip over the summit of the famous seven mile bank. Seven miles of 1 in 38! Who ever thought the Lickey Incline was formidable? Always inclined to exaggerate, those English. By the time we reach Talybont-on-Usk, we will have dropped 925ft from Torpantau, but we are a long way from there yet. The motion of the Mogul is a lead coloured blur as we hurtle along at what seems a highly dangerous speed until the brakes go on for Pentir Rhiw. To anyone without local knowledge, this tiny station would appear to have been put there just to test the brakes, but the village it was built to serve lies under the waters of the Talybont Reservoir in Glyn Collwyn below. If there was another signalbox with a booking office window I never saw it and if anyone ever bought a ticket there, I never saw that either. This marked the halfway point of the bank and soon we're helter-skeltering down to the beautifully situated station at Talybont-on-Usk. A wooded canal tow path parallels the up platform and there is a gate in the iron railings giving direct access. Wild roses star the hedgerows and men fish peacefully. An old gentleman is frightening the life out of two teenaged girls with a wasps nest full of live wasps. They run squealing along the platform as a train of ICI tank wagons makes a run at the bank. The two pannier tanks at the head are blowing off vigorously and barking away like anti-aircraft guns as they get to grips with the climb. The exhausts are echoing back off the mountain sides as our Mogul chatters off towards Talyllyn Junction on a more or less level formation. Pulses return to normal now. Not for nothing was the B&M often known as the Breakneck and Murder; the Seven Mile Bank had been the scene of some spectacular runaways in the past.

And so to Talyllyn, junction for the Mid-Wales Railway, latterly worked by the Cambrian. This line had that mysteriously named junction, Three Cocks, but staying for the moment with the B&M, Talyllyn Junction was arguably the most delightful station anywhere. The junction itself was triangular, with platforms on two sides of the vee but the gem of this pretty stone-built station was on the up B&M platform. The sign of the Hobby Horse swung outside the refreshment room advertising Rhymney and Crosswells beer. Beer was served from barrels behind the bar and old fashioned sweet jars lined the counter. Another joy of Talyllyn Junction was the chance of an extended stop if a

Below:
The 11am Newport–Brecon, hauled by Ivatt Class 2 No 46518, passes Park Junction, Newport, on 23 August 1954. *S. Rickard*

troop train was about. This happened quite frequently and on this occasion we have something like 20min to enjoy the products of Messrs Rhymney and Crosswells before packed coaches, double headed by a pair '2251s', roars through. The afternoon is hot here on the valley bottom and most of the passengers (and crew) seem reluctant to resume the journey. We start again and immediately enter Talyllyn Tunnel. This was the oldest railway tunnel anywhere in Britain, if you count air space. The original tunnel had been built for a tramroad in 1816 and was enlarged for the opening of the railway in 1860. Some committee or other, formed to celebrate the Festival of Britain in 1951, had erected a plaque at the tunnel entrance, which gave its history. I wonder what became of it when the line closed.

And so to the last four miles into Brecon, calling at the GWR-built Groesffordd Halt on the way. Although the countryside is quite pleasant here, it can only come as an anticlimax after the previous spectacles and it is with an odd sense of relief that we roll to a gentle stop at Brecon. A spacious and impressive station, exuding an air of Victorian confidence, quite unjustified of course because the old B&M was always impecunious and trying to live off its richer neighbours. The large station building

on the down side had been the company headquarters. It also housed the offices of the Mid-Wales and Neath & Brecon Companies. This impressive establishment was opened in 1871 to replace two separate and smaller stations, one of its own and the other belonging to the N&B. To the left, as we arrive, is the locomotive depot with piles of sulphurous ash lying around and a man who appears to be trying to demolish a pannier tank with a 20lb hammer. The only thing that he can possibly be attempting is to straighten a coupling rod, in situ. I mentally wish him luck and cross to the down side to watch No 46512 being turned near the down bay platform. This is always a popular spectacle and a

group of passengers linger to see the performance before leaving for their homes. The sight always put me in mind of those donkeys in the Middle East that walk endlessly around wells drawing up water. It was often the source of much ribaldry among the onlookers but the crowd today are well behaved. The turntable must be well balanced because the men pushing it don't seem to be working hard and they finish the job faultlessly, fully aware of the critical gaze of the fare paying public. My watch tells me that I have just over half an hour for a bite to eat before returning at 6.15pm.

From my cafe table I hear the whistle of another Ivatt Mogul announcing the arrival of the 4.05pm ex-Hereford, followed by a what sounds like a pannier tank on the 4.10pm ex-Neath (Riverside) running about 10min late. Why this should be, I cannot imagine (unless the crew have been chasing sheep off the line, a not unusual occurrence) and I finish my tea and stroll back to the station to begin the journey home.

As always I was struck by the fact that this large station had neither footbridge nor subway to cross the line. It must surely have been the biggest

Below:
The tiny station at Pentir Rhiw on 4 September 1963, with 0-6-0PT No 9676 taking a Brecon–Merthyr freight up the gradient. *B. J. Ashworth*

without such facilities. The Mogul off the Hereford is No 46521, now of Severn Valley fame, and that man is still hammering away at the poor unfortunate pannier tank.

The journey home will be as spectacular as ever with the high hills hiding the lowering sun and turning the reservoirs to pewter, but the best time to travel back this way was in the depths of winter when braziers burned at the water columns and icicles clung to cab steps.

One such journey began for me in an unorthodox way in the winter of 1957. I had been so taken with a girl I had met in my usual cafe (I was younger then!) that I quite forgot the time and arrived breathless at the station at 6.17pm, to find the 6.15pm still in the platform and without a locomotive. Passengers were complaining about the lack of heat and I set off in search of the engine. The night was bitterly cold with freezing fog and the train engine, No 3691, was being turned. The driver told me she was not steaming very well and, much against the grain it seemed, he had asked for assistance. This duly arrived in the form of my old friend No 46521 and both engines coupled on to the train. The Ivatt's driver was a pleasant man, and in response to my question as to how he liked these locomotives, he invited me on to the footplate to see for myself. The cab seemed enormous by GWR standards and was certainly much cosier in that hostile weather.

So about 10min late we set out into the night. The Ivatt doesn't seem to be working hard but we fairly romp along to the first stop at Groesffordd where three passengers de-train and disappear into the night, coat collars turned up. By Talyllyn Junction

we've already gained a minute and smart station work sees us away in about 40sec instead of the 3min allowed. We lose some of this at Talybont on Usk as a considerable amount of parcel traffic is loaded into the van. We're off again with rapid acceleration and I look over the side to make sure the train is still following. Sure enough, the pannier tank and coaches are bucketing along behind us and we hit the foot of the 7-mile bank. To ascend the bank was a never to be forgotten experience under any conditions, but this was a night for the connoisseur. Both locomotives were working flat out and, fair play, the Pannier seemed to be doing her share of the work. The occasional light from a lonely farmstead could be seen until we ran into a snowstorm and the outside world turned white, tinged with the glow from the fireboxes. There was a quality to that climb which seems to defy description. It was as if nothing else existed in the world apart from the bucking footplate and the noise made by these two gallant locomotives. Sparks shot high into the air from both chimneys and vanished abruptly as the snow extinguished them. If anyone thought they saw unidentified flying objects in Breconshire that night, let me assure them it was us! I never accepted a footplate ride without offering to do my share of the work and

Below:
On 2 May 1964 the Stephenson Locomotive Society ran a Cardiff–Brecon railtour, double-headed by preserved '4500' 2-6-2T No 4555 and '5700' 0-6-0PT No 3690. The train is seen during a stop for water in the attractive setting of Talybont. *J. Goss*

Above:
A pair of '2251' 0-6-0s, Nos 2242 and 2249, leave Three Cocks Junction on 24 May 1959 with a Newcastle–Brecon troop train. *D. S. Fish*

this was no exception. The fireman handed me the shovel and I set to work. The shovel felt like a toy after the much larger Great Western version but I found this locomotive a joy to fire. The fire was even and fairly thick – that's the way he liked it, the fireman informed me – and by the way she was throwing sparks, I think anything thinner would have left us with an empty grate and some embarrassing questions on the carpet. But how that engine could steam! I wonder if the present owners find it so undemanding. We stopped at Pentir Rhiw with the glow from the oil lamps in the signalbox barely discernible through the driving snow. Here I relinquished the shovel and we continued the climb in like manner. I couldn't see a thing ahead of us so it was quite a surprise when the blower was put on and we entered Torpantau Tunnel and went over the hump to emerge at the dimly lit station. Here the Ivatt came off and ran forward into the relief sidings and I went to the comfort of the cushions. Less exciting, of course, but much more comfortable. We were just a minute late and from now on it was all downhill so there wouldn't be any more worries for the driver of No 3691. The two engines exchanged whistles as we set off into the darkness. They had certainly been making steam because my compartment was piping hot. The last thing I remember was the glow in the sky that marked Merthyr Tydfil. I nodded off to be woken by the guard at Newport. I was in the middle of a dream about pretty girls in tea rooms who drove Ivatts while I slaved away dutifully with the shovel!

The loss of the Brecon & Merthyr lines in the early 1960s left a gap that no other railway could fill. Only the West Highland could rival it for scenery and that couldn't be visited in an afternoon from South Wales. If only the B&M had lived on for a few more years. Still, all is not lost and Tony Hills intends to run his Brecon Mountain Railway on from Pontsticill through the old Torpantau Tunnel to a new station overlooking Glyn Collwyn, right at the top of the 7-mile bank. Tantalising, isn't it? Who knows but one day Pentir Rhiw might again echo to the sound of steam, even if it is a narrow gauge Baldwin Pacific.

Below:
The 1.25pm Brecon–Moat Lane Junction emerges from Talyllyn Tunnel behind Ivatt 2-6-0 No 46518 on 2 May 1959. *S. Rickard*

Right:
Brecon station in the late 1950s. Ivatt 2-6-0 No 46522 awaits departure with the 2.05pm for Newport.
R. E. Toop

Below:
Climbing away from Pentir Rhiw on 27 May 1959, a Brecon–Newport train is headed by '5700' 0-6-0PT No 3662. *D. S. Fish*

Kuala Lumpur in Camera

Railways reached Malaysia towards the end of the 19th century and one of the first sections to open, in 1886, ran southwards from Kuala Lumpur for 20 miles to Kajang. The impressive station serving the Malaysian capital was built in that year; these photographs were taken there in August 1984.

Above:
Japanese-built diesel No 22124 *Tangjom Malim* arrives at Kuala Lumpur from the north with the 08.30 from Butterworth. The train was loaded to 13 vehicles and is one of the few that carries air-conditioned stock and all three classes of Malaysian rail travel.   *J. R. P. Fraser*

Below:
In 1955, 26 main line diesels were ordered as part of the Malaysian Railways modernisation scheme. One of these, built by English Electric, No 20104 *Bunga Melor* trundles towards the station from the depot, situated on the far side of the road bridge.
J. R. P. Fraser

Above:
The empty stock of the 08.30 from Butterworth is taken to the carriage sidings by No. 19104.
J. R. P. Fraser

Below:
A freight passes through Kuala Lumpur station hauled by No 22126 *Merlinau*. Malaysian main line locomotives carry their nameplates beneath the cabside windows. *J. R. P. Fraser*

Top:
A general view of part of the locomotive depot at Kuala Lumpur. In 1984, Malaysian Railways operated 91 main line diesels, 41 shunting locomotives and 22 railcars. *J. R. P. Fraser*

Above:
Steam traction officially ended in 1975 but many locomotives remained at the depots. No 562.04 is one of two steam locomotives still at Kuala Lumpur. *J. R. P. Fraser*

Left:
Evidence of squatters in residence at the carriage sidings! The sight of people using the yards for washing at the hand-pumps or cooking supper over an open fire was not uncommon in the evenings. *J. R. P. Fraser*

A Gricer's Travels

D. J. Mant

It was the evening of New Year's Day 1965 and No D815 *Druid* glided into Salisbury in the way that only 'Warships' could. I was a bit apprehensive as I was about to venture into unknown territory. Day trips had taken me to Bristol, Cardiff, Reading and London, but this was going to be different – a visit to steam depots in Liverpool and Manchester. The names were familiar, but the places were only points on a map. Now I was going to see them.

The rendezvous was Euston at 23.00. A big London station late at night is very different from the familiar daytime scene; just as much activity but concerned with newspaper, mail and sleeping car trains. A party of about 50 people aged from early 'teens upwards made for the Liverpool train. There was still some steam around at this time, on station pilot and empty stock duties, but all main line trains were diesel hauled and electrification was not far away. By the time we started out the excitement was beginning to make itself felt. I wondered how I would manage for sleep in an ordinary compartment. I soon found out. 'Willesden on the left!' somebody shouted, and there was a mad scramble to the window in case anything could be seen amid the billowing clouds of smoke and steam. Many locomotives were moving about but most were grimy and the numbers were difficult to read. This set the pattern for the rest of the journey, for there were several insomniacs in the party. The many nodding heads in the bus as we drove around Liverpool showed who had been running up and down the corridor all night!

On the early part of the journey BR/Sulzer Type 2s (Class 24) and English Electric Type 4s (Class 40) were the most common locomotives. Later, near Crewe, I noted 'Britannia' No 70018 *Flying Dutchman* and was quite disapointed as I had seen it previously when it was allocated to the Western Region. I had thought that once away from London every locomotive would be a 'cop'. Soon I saw my first 25kV electric locomotive, No E3003 (81.002) and excitement mounted again. On the final stage I noted many more locomotives, both diesel and steam, mainly LMS 2-6-4Ts and 'Black 5s' but including '9F' 2-10-0 No 92046. The whistling sound of our locomotive, No D331 (40.131) echoed around Lime Street as we pulled in and made the cavernous station seem very large and empty at this unearthly hour.

Below:
One of Birkenhead's allocation of Hughes/Fowler 'Crab' 2-6-0s, No 42942 builds up steam pressure at the depot on 29 July 1966. *John White*

Above:
The jackshaft drive of ex-LMS diesel shunters in the 12003-32 number series was a distinctive feature. At Speke on 18 May 1958 is the first of the type, No 12003. *P. J. Sharpe*

At the station entrance a Ribble 53-seater bus was waiting. It quickly whisked us through the still empty streets and through the Mersey Tunnel to Birkenhead. We piled out and waited in the dingy alley that leads to the depot. It was very cold, misty and still dark. From within the shed came the sounds of steam locomotives. Eventually we filed down the steps and into the shed – it was my first visit to a steam depot at night. Up and down the rows of cold locomotives we went, past 'Jinties',

Below:
Six months after the author's visit, Stanier 4-6-0s predominate at Warrington (Dallam) on 1 July 1965. 'Jubilee' No 45563 *Australia* is third from right and the Class 5s include Nos 45041 and 45442. Also on view are a 'Jinty' 0-6-0T and Standard '9F' 2-10-0s. *W. D. Ballard*

'Crabs', '8Fs', '9Fs' and 2-6-4Ts, busily noting numbers in the semi-darkness. Out into the yard, where spotlights made pools of light on the ground. A '9F' was moving in the blackness, slipping on greasy rails and causing a shower of sooty water. My new notebook was suitably christened! On we went, over piles of coal, trying to avoid the icy pools of water waiting to catch the unwary. Here was a 'WD', No 90040, which I had seen before, but there was a good 'cop' – ex-Crosti boiler fitted '9F' No 92020. Huddled together at one side of the depot were four of the Hudswell Clarke diesel mechanical shunters employed in the docks, Nos D2500/2/4/5. Many of the party looked upon all diesels with disgust, but these machines were unusual – they were even fitted with chimneys like those of steam locomotives!

Next was Speke. Many depots seem to be up back streets; here were blocks of flats which had seen better days and on the footpath were old cars that, by the look of the battered remains, were used as adventure playgrounds. On shed were more '9Fs' including another ex-Crosti, No 92024, LMS '5s'

Bolton Shed in 1965 and 1967

Left:
Stanier '5' No 44736 is reflected in the watery environment of its home depot as a visiting party of enthusiasts seek other locomotives stabled in the yard on 23 October 1965. *David Percival*

and '8Fs', 'Crabs' and Ivatt 2-6-0s of both types. On the diesel front there were several shunters including five of the ex-LMS diesel electric 0-6-0s with jackshaft drive, introduced in 1939.

By the time we reached Warrington it was getting light, although the weather remained dull, cold and misty all day. Some different types of locomotive were seen here. Six LMS '4F' 0-6-0s and one of the earlier Midland examples, No 43954, were on shed, as were Stanier 2-6-0s Nos 42950/58 and 10 'Jubilees'. Many locomotives were in store – a sight repeated at many of the depots – forlorn lines of dead locomotives with frost glistening white on top

of layers of grime. We saw the same as the bus pulled over the road bridge behind Springs Branch, Wigan, where the long lines of stored locomotives were mostly LMS types and 'WDs'. At the depot were a couple of LNER 'B1s', Nos 61056/144, and some 'Britannias' including No 70013 *Oliver Cromwell*, later preserved. The only 'Duchess' seen during the two days was here – No 46243 with its *City of Lancaster* nameplates removed. The Pacific still looked powerful, though it would never run again and, like many other locomotives here, it would soon be chunks of iron in a scrapyard.

Time now for a quick meal break in Bolton. It seems as if we have been going for ages but it is still only mid-morning. This tour was much more leisurely than some later ones, when meal breaks were regarded as taking up valuable 'shed bashing' time. After the break we visited the shed, slightly smaller than the previous one but containing some interesting locomotives. Among them were BR '2' 2-6-2Ts Nos 84017/25 and Lancashire & Yorkshire 0-6-0ST No 11305, the last of its type, which had been employed at Horwich Works.

By the time we reached Bury I was beginning to lose track of time and place as depot followed depot in growing tiredness. The steam locomotive types

Below:
'8F' 2-8-0 No 48380 and two Standard '5' 4-6-0s, one of which is No 73040, pose in the evening sun on 19 June 1967. *Michael S. Stokes*

Newton Heath in 1966 and 1967

Above:
The line-up on 27 April 1966 reflects the fact that at that time Newton Heath was one of the largest steam sheds on BR, with over 70 locomotives allocated. *Ian Smith*

were much the same as at other depots but here were some of the Manchester-Bury electric multiple-units (Class 504). 'Huh, electric bug carts', someone was heard to exclaim. But I had not seen these units before so at least I had a quick look at them, with their odd system of side contact third-rail pick-up. Sutton Oak, at St Helens, was only a small depot but again some interesting locomotives were present. BR '4' 2-6-0s No 76078/79 were part

Below:
More than 50 steam locomotives remained on 18 March 1967 when this view shows 'Black 5' 4-6-0s Nos 45255, 45411 and 45222 in company with '8F' No 48533. *Ian G. Holt*

of a batch of four allocated, the only members of the class in the area at the time; another Midland '4F', No 43994, was found; and an Ivatt '2' 2-6-2T No 41286 was on shed.

I looked forward to Edge Hill, the main shed in the division. But most of the express passenger work had obviously ended and there was the usual air of decay. However, the first locomotive we saw was one of the few named LMS '5s', No 45156 *Ayrshire Yeomanry*, and also on shed was 'Royal Scot' No 46152 *The King's Dragoon Guardsman* which I had seen a few years before at Kentish Town. There was not much more of note – I was getting used to rows of 'Black 5s', '8Fs', 'Jinties' and 'Crabs'. Aintree caused a problem for our driver as the shed was approached by a cinder path with a double bend over and under railway bridges. It would have been quicker to walk down the path but the 36ft bus eventually squeezed around the corners and into the depot car park. Among the usual array of steam locomotives was one of the small Yorkshire Engine Co (Class 02) diesel shunters, No D2852.

At Bank Hall was the familiar line of stored steam locomotives. Among the others were four more 'Jubilees' and another two Yorkshire Engine Co shunters. By now we were at the end of a tiring day and a bus load of sleepy gricers made for the Liverpool YMCA. Some participants seemed to have gained a second wind and talked of finding a local hostelry; I was just about ready to sleep for 12 hours! This was yet another sign of how leisurely the tour was – later ones had a coach with two drivers and kept going all night. Not all shed foremen, though, reacted kindly to a party of gricers descending upon them at 3am!

Not so bright, but early next morning we were on the road to Manchester, and Newton Heath. The large diesel multiple-unit allocation at this sizeable depot was much scorned by the organisers, but I noted parcels car No M55988 and diesel shunters Nos D2859/66 by the diesel depot before becoming engulfed in rows of steam locomotives. Most of the common types were represented and 'Britannia' No 70049 *Solway Firth* was also noted. At Gorton there was little evidence of the old Great Central, the only LNER locomotives being two withdrawn 'B1s', Nos 61269/369. Three Fowler 2-6-4Ts, Nos 42327/34/68 were here, along with several Midland and LMS '4Fs' and many 'Crabs' including the pioneer No 42700, later preserved. Two of the LMS jackshaft drive 0-6-0s, Nos 12010/24, were among the diesel shunters on view. Longsight greeted us with a line of electric locomotives by the entrance. In the steam depot were a variety of LMS types and a 'WD' 2-8-0.

More of the, by now, familiar classes were present at Heaton Mersey depot in Stockpot and a '9F', No 92131 was also on shed. Stockport Edgeley, a few minutes away, adjacent to the town's main station, was more interesting. The first

Above:
The atmosphere of a steam shed is captured in this scene at Heaton Mersey on 23 March 1967.
Michael S. Stokes

Below:
'Britannia' Pacific No 70039 *Sir Christopher Wren* is minus its nameplates at Stockport Edgeley on 16 September 1965. *J. W. Perry*

two locomotives we saw required careful recording – Ivatt '2' No 46523 and 'Jubilee' No 45632 *Tonga*! Double chimney 'Jubilee' No 45596 *Bahamas*, later preserved, and three BR '2' 2-6-2Ts, Nos 84013/14/26 were among the locomotives present. Visitors from the North Eastern Region were 'B1' No 61023 *Hirola*, based at Low Moor, and '4F' No 44408 from Normanton.

After Stockport came Agecroft which seemed to be in the middle of nowhere with only coal mines for company; I was completely lost anyway and I think the bus driver was at times, too! The locomotives here included a couple of 'Jinties' and the later preserved '8F' No 48773. Patricroft was a rather unusual depot, having two shed buildings in an 'L' shape with the turntable and coaling plant between them. One main line diesel, No D274 (40.074) glinted in the brief watery sunshine amidst rows of steam locomotives and the only other diesels here were a few 0-6-0 (Class 08) shunters. The large allocation included some BR '5s' with Caprotti valve gear. In fact, my *Locoshed Book* told me that Nos 73125-44 were based here and the other 10 Caprottis were in Scotland. 17 of the Patricroft batch were seen, although some appeared to be stored in one section of the shed, which was as quiet as a graveyard as the party filed up and down the lines of locomotives.

Several BR/Sulzer Type 2 diesels (later Class 25) were in evidence at Trafford Park, along with a couple of 'Peaks', but the steam side was no less interesting. 'Black 5' No 44661, looking quite presentable, posed for photographs outside the shed and the depot contained more of the same class, '4Fs', '8Fs', Ivatt '4' 2-6-0s, 2-6-4Ts and a 'Crab'. This was our last depot and we made our way back to Piccadilly station, where I was

Above:
A November evening in 1967 finds Stockport Edgeley mainly occupied by 'Black 5s' including Nos 45073 and 45221. *J. B. Mounsey*

Below:
The fireman prepares to dismount and reset the points as '8F' No 48536 moves through the yard at Agecroft on 23 October 1965. *David Percival*

delighted to see one of the 'EM2' 1,500V dc Co-Cos (later Class 77), No 27005 *Minerva*.

After all the rushing around of the two days, the journey home seemed rather an anti-climax. We had electric locomotive No E3045 (84.010) for the first part of the journey and No D333 (40.133) on the second stage. At Waterloo, and once more in familiar territory, I found No D815 again on my Exeter train.

Back home, I analysed my notes and found I had seen 643 locomotives for the first time – a good score. The outlay was £4.15s (£4.75) and we had visited 18 depots of which I think 12 are no longer in existence. Many of the locomotives were of large classes of LMS and BR Standard types but, even in 1965, a few 'old timers' had been seen. How I wish I had made this tour earlier – what might I have seen

Above:

Nameplates, numberplates and shedplates were removed from many locomotives towards the end of the steam era. At Patricroft on 5 May 1968, Standard 'Caprotti 5' No 73125 has a replacement wooden numberplate and painted 'shedplate'. *N. E. Preedy*

then! No good wishing, though, the next tour is to the North East in the spring. I had better get my application in as soon as possible, for the LNER section of my *Locoshed Book* looks very bare!

Below:

Devoid of its hose, the water crane will not, in any case, be required by the '8F' standing alongside at Trafford Park on 20 August 1967, for No 48535 was withdrawn earlier in the month. 'Black 5' 4-6-0s Nos 44708 and 44834 will soldier on a little longer.
David Percival

Galway Bay Railtour

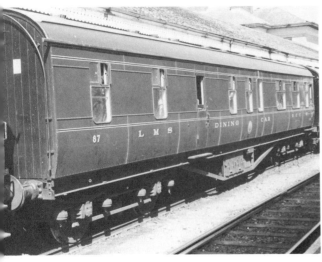

The Railway Preservation Society of Ireland's annual two-day railtour in 1984 saw action from 'S' 4-4-0 No 171 *Slieve Gullion* and 'J15' 0-6-0 No 184. Conducted at a leisurely pace, the railtour featured numerous photographic stops, train splitting, run-pasts and lineside bus excursions – all affording participants with plenty of photographic opportunities.

Above:
Slieve Gullion takes water during a lengthy stop at Athlone during the outward journey on 12 May. CIE Class 141 Bo-Bo diesel electric No 144 is visible at the opposite side of the platform.　*David Percival*

Left:
Newly restored UTA-built dining car No 87, in LMS/NCC livery – one of three vehicles in the train which were mentioned in the citation for the Association of Railway Preservation Societies' annual award held by the RPSI in 1984.　*A. White*

Above:
'J15' 0-6-0 No 184 blackens the sky on 12 May 1984
with a run past at Castlegrove on the freight only line
from Claremorris to Athenry. The 0-6-0 joined the
railtour at Claremorris and took five coaches over this
route to Galway while No 171 and the remaining two
returned to Mullingar before proceeding to Galway
over the direct route.   *David Percival*

Right:
Storming past photographers at Castlerea — 4-4-0 No
171 *Slieve Gullion* makes a run past on the outward
journey.   *David Percival*

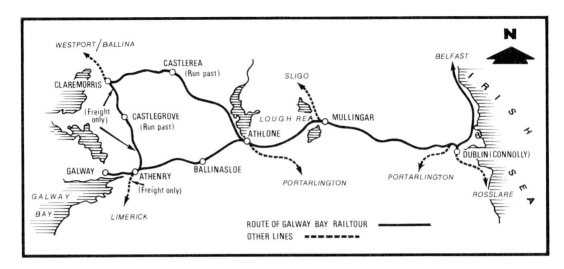

ROUTE OF GALWAY BAY RAILTOUR ———
OTHER LINES ─ ─ ─ ─ ─

Left:
On the second day, 'J15' No 184 prepares to leave Galway at 08.55 with the first, three-coach portion of the railtour. *Slieve Gullion* waits to collect its stock for the 09.45 departure.   *A. White*

Below:
The two portions of the 'Galway Bay Railtour' on 13 May come together for the first time at Athenry, where No 171 went ahead after a brief stop alongside the waiting No 184.   *David Percival*

Above:
After No 184 gained the lead once more at Attymon Junction, the two portions combined at Ballinasloe. The complete train is seen here as it approaches Ballinasloe station before continuing with both locomotives in charge as far as Mullingar, where No 184 ended its duty and retired to the RPSI depot. *David Percival*

Below:
At Mullingar, the RPSI's southern base, former Dublin & South Eastern inside-cylindered express goods 2-6-0 No 15 (later No 461) awaits restoration. *A. White*

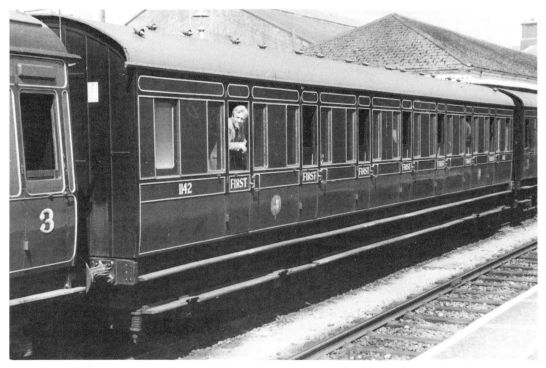

Above:
Another of the splendidly restored vehicles which helped to win the ARPS award, corridor first No 1142 dates from 1914 and made its debut on RPSI main line work in 1984. *A. White*

Below:
No 171 *Slieve Gullion* speeds through Balbriggan on the evening of 13 May on its way from Dublin to Belfast (thence to the RPSI headquarters at Whitehead next day), providing extra mileage for many of the railtour passengers. *David Percival*

Stafford in the 1950s

Brian Morrison

To be fair, it was February. It was raining and it was cold, but Stafford station just did not look anything at all like it did when I was there in the 1950s. The shed building was all that remained of the once-busy depot, the coaling tower had vanished, the station buildings were of recent times and a plethora of overhead 'knitting' did its best to obscure what little photographic light there was. A few Class 86 electric locomotives, a Class 47 diesel and a multiple-unit . . . and little incentive to remain any longer. It was a very different story in the late 1950s.

Then, it was summer. The sun was shining and it was pleasantly warm, and the scene generally appeared anything but antiseptic, as it does now. There was no electric traction and only a few diesels, but they were not missed, for the camera was pointed at a seemingly endless procession of a variety of steam locomotives.

My first look at Stafford was on 7 August 1956, having travelled by train from Shrewsbury. I had no sooner alighted when 'Patriot' 4-6-0 No 45503 *The Royal Leicestershire Regiment* pulled away with a semi-fast for Crewe and 'Duchess' Pacific No 46240 *City of Coventry* stormed through on an express for Carlisle. 'Royal Scot' 4-6-0 No 46162 *Queen's Westminster Rifleman* quickly followed with a 'fast' for Blackpool, and Fairburn 2-6-4T No 42233 departed with the 1.58pm local service to Stoke-on-Trent. An old Midland Railway 0-6-0, No 43709 lumbered by with a heavy haul of plate wagons

Stafford – 7 August 1956:

Below:
'Jinty' 0-6-0T No 47649 shunts the yard to the south of the station, a duty that was soon to be taken over by a Class 08 diesel shunter. *Brian Morrison*

Above:
Stainier 2-6-0 No 42950 heads home for Crewe South with a mixed freight from Wolverhampton, passing a couple of gangers on the left and the shed yards on the right. Fowler Class 4MT 2-6-4T No 42347 is in the background. This is one of the author's favourite photographs of the period. *Brian Morrison*

containing concrete slabs and was no sooner out of sight than the 2.20pm for Manchester left the station behind another Fairburn tank, No 42151. The inevitable 'Black 5' then put in an appearance, hauling a down freight; No 45282 was well worth an exposure as it was in ex-works condition after a visit to Crewe. Although minus its locomotive headboard, the down 'Red Rose' for Liverpool was easily identifiable by the destination boards above the windows of the smart array of maroon coaches, headed by No 46244 *King George VI*.

Just 40 Stanier Moguls were constructed in the early 1930s and I was very pleased that the next train through on the goods avoiding line was No 42950 of the class, as they were not at all commonplace before my camera. In fact, this particular photograph remains one of my personal favourites – the gangers, signals, four-wheeled wagons and Fowler 2-6-4T in the background all adding up to a scene that was the epitome of our country's steam railway system at that time.

The scene changed rapidly. 'Jubilee' 4-6-0 No 45617 *Mauritius* and 'Black 5' No 44902 arrived, double-heading a Birmingham-Manchester service, and Pacific No 46239 *City of Chester* charged through with the down 'Royal Scot'. A variety of passenger turns during the next hour presented 'Patriot' No 45520 *Llandudno* and 'Jubilees' Nos 45700 *Amethyst*, 45734 *Meteor*, double-chimneyed 45736 *Phoenix* and 45552 *Silver Jubilee* herself. Their passage was interspersed with a mixed bag of freight trains hauled by 'Black 5s', '8Fs', tank engines of many types and ex-LNWR 0-8-0 No 49119. A Class 2P 4-4-0 put in an appearance on the local service to Crewe, which otherwise was in the capable hands of Fowler, Stanier and Fairburn 2-6-4Ts. The day was a pleasant one and the resultant prints were good.

It was another August day, in 1958, when I next returned to Stafford and although the weather was once more sunny and warm, the day was interrupted by heavy showers. An entirely different viewpoint was selected, to avoid duplication of photographs and to afford a better background for southbound trains. The signalman in the South box was very amenable and a number of exposures were made from the steps of his domain.

Highlights of this day were No 46228 *Duchess of Rutland* with the up 'Royal Scot'; one of only four named 'Black 5s', No 45156 *Ayrshire Yeomanry* with a down freight; a 'Black 5' piloting 'Royal Scot' No 46112 *Sherwood Forester* on the 15 bogies that

Left:
Stanier '8F' 2-8-0 No 48035 has steam to spare passing through the station with empty plate wagons heading north. *Brian Morrison*

Stafford – August 1956:

Above:

With the shed yards to the right, ex-LNWR Class G2a 0-8-0 No 49119 steams freely passing through with a freight typical of the day and heads back home to Warrington. In the background, Fowler '2P' 4-4-0 No 40580 and an Ivatt Mogul queue for their turn under the coaling tower. *Brian Morrison*

formed the up 'Welshman'; and the prototype *Deltic* speeding through with the 'Manxman' from Liverpool. By this date a start had been made with dieselisation of local services and I photographed what was to become a Class 104 diesel multiple-unit working the 2.35pm to Birmingham New Street.

I intend to return to Stafford again to try and obtain some pictorial photographs of the current scene. This time I will be fair and select a sunny day. Even with today's cameras and lenses, however, I somehow doubt that very much will stir the blood as did the steam parade of the 1950s. As a contemporary of mine says, however, there is the challenge!

Stafford – August 1958:

Below:

The most prestigious train of the day between Glasgow and London is still the 'Royal Scot'. Storming through Stafford, a rather grimy 'Duchess' Pacific No 46228 *Duchess of Rutland* heads a smart rake of maroon coaching stock. *Brian Morrison*

Left:
A summer storm is in progress as one of only four named 'Black 5s' No 45156 *Ayrshire Yeomanry* approaches the station with a down van train.
Brian Morrison

Below:
'Black 5' No 45147 pilots 'Royal Scot' No 46112 *Sherwood Forester* away from the scheduled Stafford stop with the 15 bogies that made up the 'Welshman' titled train, a service that carried through coaches from Portmadoc (Porthmadog as it is now known), Pwllheli and Llandudno for Euston where it was scheduled to arrive at 6.25pm. *Brian Morrison*

Bottom:
Resplendent in light blue with white-lined decoration markings, the prototype *Deltic* roars through the station with the up 'Manxman' from Liverpool. *Brian Morrison*

Leighton Buzzard Gala Day

Featuring some half-a-dozen assorted steam locomotives and an equally varied collection of industrial diesels, the Leighton Buzzard Narrow Gauge Railway is a 2ft gauge delight in semi-rural Bedfordshire. These photographs were taken at a Gala Day on 24 June 1984.

Below:
Baguley 0-4-0T of 1921, No 3 *Rishra* runs through recent housing developments at Leighton Buzzard on the approach to Pages Park with a lightweight morning train.   *Keith Smith*

Above:
It would be hard to find anything more basic in terms of narrow gauge diesel traction than this – although weather protection of sorts is provided! A 1939-vintage Lister diesel, No 16 *Thorin Oakenshield* heads a demonstration train at Stonehenge, comprising three of the tipper wagons formerly used for the line's sand traffic. *Keith Smith*

Left:
Leaving Stonehenge, Orenstein & Koppel 0-6-0WT No 5 *Elf,* built in 1936, sets out on the 2-mile journey to Pages Park. *Keith Smith*

Below:
The 1922-built Kerr Stuart 0-4-0ST No 2 *Pixie* receives assistance from one of the railway's Simplex diesels on an afternoon working. The extra power will be welcome as the heavily-loaded train has one or two difficult inclines to conquer. *Keith Smith*

Below:
Centenarian No 1 *Chaloner* – the de Winton vertical-boilered 0-4-0 dating from 1877 – is prepared at Pages Park depot on the morning of Gala Day. Behind it, *Rishra* raises steam and, alongside, *Pixie* and *Elf* are ready for the day's work. *Keith Smith*

Bottom:
Outside Stonehenge workshops are three Simplexes (Nos 10 *Haydn Taylor* and No 12 *Carbon* in the foreground) and a Ruston diesel. Simplex diesels hauled the line's sand trains in its working days. *Keith Smith*

The Iron Dragon

Dr Peter Jarvis

The Great Wall of China has been restored for a mile on either side of the great gate at Badaling. It rises by swoops and swirls to the skyline, quite as steeply as a Welsh slate quarry incline, and it is teeming with friendly people. They tell you they have been studying English from the radio and they marvel at your big nose and round eyes. Chinese eyes are far more practical in the dusty climate of North China, as you find when you walk from one tower to the next into the hilltop winds. A mournful camel is photographed with everybody's children; terrified girl soldiers clamber down the wallwalk, knuckles blanched on the handrail. Fortunately there are steps when the gradient becomes 1 in 1! At last you reach the top of the climb, the restored section of wall stops, and you march on broken stones between shattered battlements along a skyline of irregularly rising hills. Here the Wall has

lost its face and half its contents down a slope; there an earthquake has cracked a tower. You can stride out with relief onto genuine archaeology, and few visitors care to try the walk. For the first time since you came to China, you can be alone.

It was here that the sound of my feet on the smashed slate of the wall top was drowned in a fearsome wailing noise. It wavered up and down across half an octave, exceedingly loud, echoing around the mountains. Mongol horsemen riding to the attack? The view northward showed nothing untoward. Did the Roman bucinae, used to terrify the Picts, sound like this? Wrong wall! Perhaps I had imagined . . . no, it came again, even louder, fierce and menacing, proud and terrible. Smoothing down the hair on the back of my neck, I looked about. At last I saw a steep gulch running down from the Wall, and at the bottom a little bridge crossing it, carrying a pair of rails.

Presently there came a great black tender, a high-perched cab and a prodigiously long boiler, with five red, white-tyred wheels beneath, then a pair of highly polished smoke deflectors and again that formidable howl. It was my first introduction to the 'Qian Jin'.

Below:
The Great Wall winds across hilltops in the Nankou Pass, north of Peking. A standard Class DF4 'Dongfeng' 4,000hp diesel-electric locomotive brings a train into Qinglongqiao in September 1978.
M. G. Howard

The 'QJ' – as it is labelled on its smokebox door – is the only steam locomotive in the world in regular production. The Chinese, well aware of this, are proud of it. We called at Datong Locomotive Works and at the tea ceremony before we began our tour, the Chief Clerk received us. 'Welcome', he said, 'to the largest and most modern steam locomotive plant in the world'.

'Greetings,' we replied, 'from the workers of the Festiniog Railway – we have the smallest and oldest . . .' and everybody fell about laughing.

Datong's casting was fairly rough, their machining was a deal better, and their welding was neat. Some girls were in charge of large lathes; the Chief Clerk said they valued the ladies for their conscientiousness and reliability; just as on the FR. It was fascinating to see vast jigs for turning 20ft fireboxes end for end, and a little astonishing to see six or seven completed fireboxes of this size littering the shop floor. Production is of one locomotive each working day, 300 a year. There are 8,000 staff whose average wage is equivalent to £25 a month – rates vary from £17 a month to the works manager who gets £75 a month. An apartment on the campus costs £3 a month.

There were people with no toetectors, no gloves and no goggles in places where these would be compulsory in Britain. When the Chief Clerk asked if we had any comradely criticism, we told him. He looked uncomfortable and said: 'Yes, these things are provided but the men won't wear them.' We said: 'In our country, if you don't wear them, you don't get a job.' We gathered he had heard these sentiments before.

Below:
A 'QJ' 2-10-2 in full cry! On 28 November 1980, No 1972 approaches Lu-Kou-Ch'iao, Peking, with a lengthy freight. *H. N. James*

They build no narrow gauge engines, and in their circumstances we thought it impracticable for them to build a one-off job. But they would be very happy to sell us a 'QJ', or if that were too large, then a nice little JS Class 2-8-2 about the size of a '9F'. As six steam engines can be built for the price of one diesel, and there are vast reserves of coal and little oil in China, the production of these splendid machines may be expected to continue for years.

We came to know the 'QJ' quite well. The overnight sleeper from Peking was sent forth up the plain with a pair of Co-Co diesels but at Datong, with serious business ahead over the mountain line to Taiyuan, they removed the diesels and replaced them with just one steam engine – a 'QJ'. The standard passenger train in China seems to consist of 13 carriages, each some 80ft long and weighing 72ton. They stand 16ft high and are 10 or 11ft wide; headroom inside is 9ft 6in. They are painted green, with two horizontal yellow stripes at window level, and to see a train wriggling along a ledge through one of the many river gorges is reminiscent of nothing so much as a great snake sliding along.

This likeness has obviously not escaped the Chinese railway engineers; the snake, it seems, is the origin of legends about dragons, and it pleases the Chinese greatly to have dragons about the place. In any large garden you will find a splendid ceramic creature writhing along the top of a wall, and when you reach the leading end, there is a most fierce head. Now, at Datong there is little to do in the evenings except drink *mao-tai* (a vile and potent rice spirit) and have dragon dreams, so naturally it follows that they like dragon heads on their Great Snake. The Chinese for a locomotive is *Tie Lung* – literally 'Iron Dragon' – so the locomotives of the Chinese National Railways are classified into the three basic types of dragon, according to the number of coupled axles.

Above:
At Hsu-Chou locomotive depot on 8 December 1980 is Class JS 'Jian She' 2-8-2 No 6061.   *H. N. James*

The Three-toed Japanese or Pacific Dragon seems to be the usual express engine such as the 'Ren Min' ('People') Pacifics. These have a delicately modulated pair of whistles tuned a fourth apart in the Chinese manner.

The Four-toed or common Chinese Dragon is a 2-8-2 maid of all work. These 'JF' ('Liberation') and 'JS' ('Construction') classes of some 2,000hp are mostly used as colliery shunters and the like. They have melodious single toned hooters which may be admired all night in the neighbourhood of shunting yards.

The Five-toed Chinese Imperial Dragon is that largest and most powerful of their locomotives, the 'QJ' or 'Forward' class. It is a 2-10-2 weighing close to 140ton with an 83ton tender on four or six axles. The 'QJ' has 5ft drivers, 3ft 5in pony wheels and a continuous rating of 3,000hp with a starting tractive effort of about 63,500lb – much the same as a BR Class 47. It is economically fired with poor quality slack by a mechanical feed. I never saw one produce more than the very faintest grey haze, even when working hard, and normally they produce no smoke at all. They are also very quiet.

The duties of the 'QJ', apart from pulling passenger trains of close on 1,000ton, are in hauling coal. Chinese coal trains come as standard rakes of 50 wagons, each of 50 or 60ton gross weight. A standard coal train therefore weighs between 2,500 and 3,000ton and we saw these pulled by one 'QJ'.

Class RM 'Ren Min' Pacific No 1154, built in 1960, at Jinan on 6 December 1980.   *H. N. James*

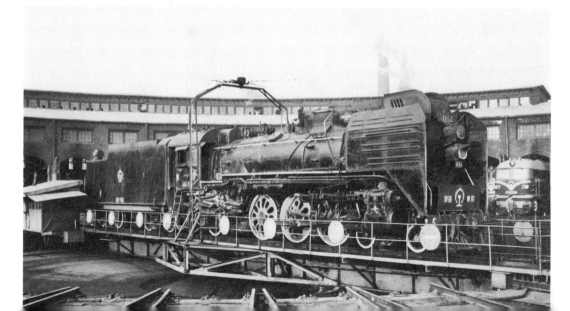

Above:
Four-toed Dragons of two types at Tangshan on 13 July 1976. 'JF' No 4007 runs past light engine in the centre while No 4008 of the same class shunts coal wagons. Alongside the platform is the station pilot, Class JS No 5096. *David M. Scudamore*

Lying in our soft sleeper trundling at a stately 50mph through the night, we could tell the class of the engines we met at every passing loop. The melodious servitude of the 2-8-2s and the polite command of the Pacifics came graciously through our slumbers, but the imperious yowl of a 'QJ' 10ft from my head woke me smartly enough – it is as well there was plenty of headroom over the top bunk!

I went to our guest lecturer, a distinctly non-railway historian, and asked: 'What kind of a noise does a Chinese Dragon make?' She gave me a Paddingtonian hard stare, and eventually replied:

'In the Gorges of the Yangzi, the wind funnels through the narrows and howls uncannily in the night. Nobody who has heard it ever forgets it, and nobody who has not been there could imagine such a terrifying noise.' The local people, sleeping happily by their stoves, attribute this noise to the most powerful and most benevolent of animals. 'It is a fortunate sign,' they say, pulling their padded jackets closer round their necks. 'The Dragons are out tonight.'

Acknowledgements and thanks are due to Mr Brian Hollingsworth for information and advice, and to Miss Hilary Jarvis for her Chinese translations.

Below:
An immaculate 'QJ', No 1555 at Tientsin on 13 July 1976. *David M. Scudamore*

View point on Bridges

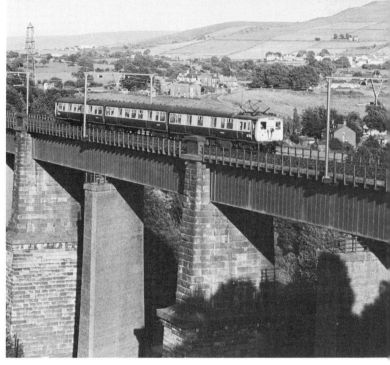

For obvious reasons, bridges and viaducts are focal points in many pictures of the railway scene. In these pages we show how photographers have approached the subject from both traditional and less-conventional angles.

Above:
Led by motor open brake second No M59407M, a Class 506 EMU crosses Broadbottom Viaduct forming the 18.58 Hadfield–Manchester Piccadilly on 20 July 1984. This 1,500V dc system was converted to 25kV ac at the end of that year and the units replaced by Class 303s. *Kim Fullbrook*

Below:
Against a backdrop of London's familiar but changing skyline, Class 415 (4-EPB) No 5221 crosses the Thames on its way out of Charing Cross as the 11.52 service to Dartford via Bexleyheath on 14 September 1977. *Brian Morrison*

Above:
An IC125 crosses the Royal Border Bridge, Berwick, on 23 April 1984. *Colin Boocock*

Below:
Crossing the River Neath and the Tennent Canal on 9 September 1977, IC125 No 253.012 forms the 15.15 Paddington–Swansea. *Les Bertram*

Above:
The Queensferry tower of the Baker and Fowler masterpiece bridging the Forth, viewed at low tide with a Class 47 heading a northbound train on the afternoon of 22 October 1983. *David Wilcock*

Below:
Dent Head Viaduct on the Settle & Carlisle, as '47' No 47.479 crosses with the 16.00 Leeds–Carlisle on 9 June 1984. *G. S. Cutts*

Above:
The Hertfordshire Railtours 'Britannia Belle' of 10 December 1983, hauled by Class 45 No 45.111 *Grenadier Guardsman,* crosses the Manchester Ship Canal at Thelwall, near Warrington. *Kim Fullbrook*

Below :
A Class 47 crosses Culloden Viaduct on 29 August 1981 with the 10.35 Inverness—Euston 'Clansman'. *P. J. Wylie*

Above:
Contrasting styles at Runcorn, where the M6 motorway bridges the Mersey alongside the railway. Class 81 No 81.003 heads the 16.08 Birmingham–Liverpool on 16 September 1981. *Brian Morrison*

Below:
The Class 45-hauled 16.00 Leeds–Carlisle crosses Ribblehead Viaduct against a menacing autumn evening sky on 16 October 1983. *Nick Dodson*

The Sandy & Potton Railway

J. M. Tolson

One of the oldest locomotives in the British Isles is the diminutive 0-4-0 well tank *Shannon*. Well known for its association with the Wantage Tramway, its working life spanned almost 90 years and began in June 1857 on the Sandy & Potton Railway, a private line in Bedfordshire, opened the same month. The major events in *Shannon's* long life are well documented and will be touched on later, but the story of the short independent existence of the S&P, and of the man who financed its construction, is equally fascinating.

The Great Northern Railway had opened the southern section of its main line as far north as Peterborough in 1850, and one of the early stations was at Sandy. Some two years later William Peel, third son of Sir Robert Peel, former Prime Minister and founder of the Metropolitan Police Force, came to live in a small house about a mile from the railway. William Peel, born in 1824, had already had a distinguished Royal Navy career, rising to the rank of Captain, by which title he was habitually known. He travelled extensively in Africa and other parts of the world, while for his valour in the Crimean War he became one of the earliest recipients of the Victoria Cross.

Despite his almost continual absence from home, Captain Peel was very interested in the wellbeing of his estates, and in the possibilities which the opening of the GN main line brought to the area. He already had some half-formed plans for a railway in mind when he purchased about 1,400 acres of relatively poor agricultural land between the railway at Sandy and Potton, a small town some three miles to the east. Some of this land was cleared and put to cultivation, but a railway line was in due course projected between the two towns, and in the Captain's absence, his agent, Mr Tilcock, was charged with working out the details. As the railway ran mainly over Peel's own land, and only a further eight acres had to be purchased, it could be built without the statutory authority of an Act of Parliament.

Construction of the line, which was about 3½ miles in length and connected with the GN main

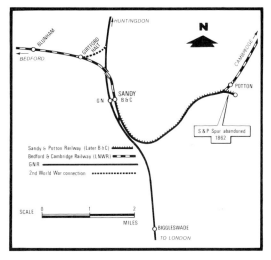

line on the Biggleswade side of Sandy, began in 1856. Benjamin Shaw Brundell of Doncaster was appointed engineer, but the contractor was a local man, Mr Culshaw of Biggleswade. The GN permitted the line to start in the station yard on the east side of the main line, provided that Captain Peel would remove it if the GN ever required the site for its own use. After passing through the yard for some distance, the S&P line then curved round the southern edge of what is now a nature reserve and the headquarters of the Royal Society for the Protection of Birds, before heading northeastwards to a terminus at the southern end of Potton. A coal yard, goods shed and engine shed were built there ready for the opening of the railway.

To work the line, a 15ton 0-4-0WT with 3ft driving wheels and 9in x 12in cylinders was purchased for £800 from George England & Company of Hatcham Iron Works, New Cross. It ran its first trip on the Sandy & Potton Railway on 17 June 1857, when it was named *Shannon* (after Captain Peel's 50-gun steam frigate) by the Captain's mother, Lady Peel.

But the main celebrations took place on 23 June. A marquee was erected near the Shambles in

121

Potton and 400 people sat down to a first class lunch which, although free for invited guests, was available to the public at 2s 6d (12½p) a head, including a pint of beer. The 44 labourers who helped build the line were also provided with lunch, and even the GN entered into the spirit of the occasion by arranging a special stop for one of its up trains at Sandy.

Shannon made a round trip from Potton hauling a coach load of friends and guests, after the representative of George England & Co, who was superintending the operations, had a narrow escape from scalding when a steam hose burst while he was struggling to get water from the well at the engine shed. At Potton the guests were conducted by the band of the Bedfordshire Militia from the station to the Market Place en route to their lunch. The cost of £96. 2s 6d for the event covered, among other things, meals for the guests, six guineas (£6.30) for the glee singers, £5 for the band, and the princely sum of £2 12s 11d (£2.65) for illuminations and handbills to publicise the event locally. The event was of such importance that it was covered by the *Illustrated London News*.

Freight traffic only was operated until April 1858, with the company's rolling stock consisting of a brake van, two wagons and a trolley. To haul these, there was *Shannon* and a 2-2-2 well tank *Little England*. This had been built by George England

Below:
The B & C line flyover north of Sandy on 14 February 1968. Passing beneath is a push-pull test train returning from Sandy to Doncaster, propelled by Class 37 No D6700. *David Percival*

with 9in x 12in cylinders and 4ft 6in driving wheels in 1851, and exhibited at the Great Exhibition in that year. Little is known with certainty of its subsequent career, but it seems most likely that it fell into the clutches of Isaac Watt Boulton and was broken up at his famous siding in the 1860s, as its nameplates were said to be mounted on the workshop walls.

Captain Peel was destined never to see his railway in operation, for he was by then in command of a naval brigade in India. He was awarded the KCB for meritorious service during the Mutiny, but was seriously wounded on 9 March 1858 at the second relief of Lucknow. Although he started to recover from his wounds, he contracted smallpox and died at Cawnpore on 22 April of the same year at the early age of 33. When he was wounded he was wielding a Roman sword, which had been found near Galley Hill Fort in a remarkable state of preservation, together with other relics, during the construction of his railway. Statues in Calcutta and in Sandy church still bear testimony to the high esteem in which he was held.

Although Board of Trade permission for the Sandy & Potton Railway to operate passenger services was granted on 5 November 1857, these did not appear in *Bradshaw* until April 1858, when four trains in each direction on weekdays were advertised. All trains connected with GN services at Sandy, and soon after their introduction the GN allowed through bookings from Potton to London. From time to time the GN hired locomotives to the S&P when one or both of the local line's engines was out of action. Signalling was almost non-existent, and consisted mainly of waving a red flag

when a would-be passenger from one of the farms along the line wished to board a train.

At the ceremonial opening, the chairman of the Executive Committee had expressed the hope that the local railway would branch out both to the east and to the west, but also declared that its advantages to the locality would be materially lessened if it fell into the hands of a major company. But the S&P's independence was to be shortlived for, on the death of Captain Peel, control of the line passed to his youngest brother, Arthur Wellesley Peel. Named after his godfather, the Duke of Wellington, he became prominent in political circles. He was speaker of the House of Commons from 1884 to 1895 and on his retirement was created Viscount Peel of Sandy.

Arthur Peel was soon involved in the promotion of the Bedford, Potton & Cambridge Railway. This line, some 30 miles in length, was projected to run to Cambridge from an end-on junction in Bedford with the Bedford Railway, whose line from Bletchley had been opened on 18 November 1846. The Bill for the BP&C was rejected in the 1859 Parliamentary session mainly because of the opposition of the GN, which also had ambitions of reaching both Bedford and Cambridge by means of alliances with other railways, both authorised and projected.

Below:
The 12.15 Bletchley–Cambridge arrives at the Bedford & Cambridge Railway station at Potton on 16 April 1966, formed of Derby single-unit motor brake second No M79900 paired with Derby motor composite No M79190. *David Percival*

Nevertheless the BP&C succeeded in mollifying the GN by granting the latter running powers over its line into Cambridge from the proposed junction with the Eastern Counties Railway branch from Shepreth. After a few minor amendments to the course of its own line, which was to run through both Sandy and Potton, the Bedford & Cambridge Railway, as it was by then known, was sanctioned on 6 August 1860 with powers to raise capital of £240,000 and loans of up to £80,000. The promoters found difficulty in raising the necessary capital, and were forced to appeal for a contribution of £70,000 from the LNWR which had already agreed to work the new line. This gave a major company the opportunity to gain control, and it insisted on appointing three directors out of a total of five on the joint committee, which was set up for the construction and operation of the line. Arthur Peel was one of the directors, Charles Liddell was appointed engineer and the contractor was Joseph Firbank.

The Act of Incorporation of the B&C had authorised the company to purchase, compulsorily or otherwise, 'the existing railway or tramway between Sandy and Potton.' This was done, as that line was to be an integral part of the new railway. Construction of the B&C began about April 1861, and the S&P closed at the end of the year. Its rolling stock was valued at £960, and was purchased by Joseph Firbank, who used *Shannon* on construction trains along the new railway. The B&C line from Bedford crossed the GN line by a bridge some distance north of Sandy, turning sharply south to run parallel to it before passing through the station and following the course of the S&P towards

Potton. The GN up platform was resited and rebuilt as an island with B&C trains using the eastern face, while the main B&C buildings were in due course sited on a platform to the east of the new line. Improvements were also made to the goods yard layout and the interchange facilities south of the station, with an up refuge siding laid in at the north end. At Potton a short stretch of the original S&P line, together with the terminal facilities on the Biggleswade Road, was abandoned, as the line to Cambridge turned northwards through the town, and a new and imposing through station was provided on the road to Sandy. The new line was single throughout, except for passing loops at intermediate stations, where only single platforms were provided at first, but additional facilities were built within a few months of the opening.

Below :

Far from any of its previous haunts, *Shannon* attracts admirers on 24 August 1975 at the 'Rail 150' celebrations at Shildon.   *J. M. Tolson*

The B&C directors were anxious that their new railway should benefit from any traffic generated by the Great Exhibition in London, so the ceremonial opening was fixed for Friday, 4 July 1862, when a special train of 26 new coaches made two round trips between Bedford and Cambridge for the directors and their guests. The public opening took place on the following Monday with a service of four trains in each direction on weekdays, but freight traffic did not start until 1 August 1862. Although the LNWR had really controlled the capital expenditure for its construction and was working the line as agreed, the B&C directors were anything but happy when in June 1863 Liddell estimated the final cost of construction at £370,175 – almost exactly double the first estimate of £186,000 and well in excess of the powers authorised in 1860. A period of acrimonious dispute followed, culminating in a controversial bill which received the Royal Assent on 23 June 1864. By this, the LNWR became responsible for all debts of the B&C, but was able to take over the management of the concern, which it did on 7 July of the same year.

The local company was finally absorbed by the LNWR under the Act of 5 July 1865.

Meanwhile, in 1863 when Firbank relinquished his remaining responsibilities for the construction and operation of the line, he sold *Shannon* to the LNWR who renumbered it as No 1104 in their duplicate list. *Shannon* spent two weeks on the Cromford & High Peak Railway in August 1863, but did not take kindly to the sharp curves and steep gradients, and was returned to Crewe, where it passed the next 15 years shunting around the works and station, being renumbered 1863 in January 1872.

In 1878 *Shannon* was sold and delivered for the princely sum of £365 8s 1d (£365.40) to the Wantage Tramway, a three mile long roadside line, which had been opened in 1875 to connect the small Berkshire market town of Wantage with the Great Western main line at Wantage Road. Despite its diminutive size, *Shannon* was quite a powerful locomotive, and it was this which led the Wantage Tramway to acquire it. It became No 5 on this line and was unofficially known as *Jane*.

Despite the closure of the Wantage Tramway to passengers from 1 August 1925, *Shanon* was kept busy on freight traffic until November 1943, after which it lay out of service until the complete closure of the line on 21 December 1945. The GWR purchased the locomotive for £100 at the sale of effects on 25 April 1946. It was then restored, given its original name, and mounted on a plinth at Wantage Road station in April 1948. When the station closed to all traffic on 29 March 1965, *Shannon* was stored on private premises in Wantage from November 1966 until despatched to the Great Western Society at Didcot in January 1969, where it was restored to working order and steamed for the first time on 11 October of the same year.

Below:
Another view of the 12.15 Bletchley–Cambridge, departing form Potton on 16 April 1966.
David Percival

Above:
On the last day of passenger services over the line, 30 December 1967, two pairs of Cravens DMUs arrive at Blunham on a Saturday Cambridge–Bedford working. *David Percival*

Before closing this account, it is perhaps appropriate to look at the later history of the line on which *Shannon* started its long life. Market gardening, which had already flourished in the area for some 200 years, benefited greatly from the coming of the railway, and heavy agricultural traffic, particularly potatoes, soon built up. On 6 July 1863, a siding for vegetable traffic was opened at Girtford, some distance west of Sandy, and close to where the Bedford line crossed the Great North Road. Passenger traffic, both local and between the university towns of Oxford and Cambridge, also developed rapidly in the latter half of the 19th century. Before the opening of the direct line between Cambridge and the north via March and Spalding, Sandy was used as the interchange station for passengers to and from the Eastern Counties, in preference to Peterborough, where a lengthy walk between stations was necessary.

The line between Sandy and Cambridge was doubled in the late summer of 1871, but because of the expense of widening the river bridges, the Bedford-Sandy section remained single, although the whole line benefited from the introduction of the electric train staff system in 1888.

World War 1 saw increased through traffic, although the siding at Girtford was temporarily closed as an economy measure at the beginning of 1917. At Sandy the LNWR side of the station, which had hitherto maintained its own staff, was placed under GN control. Between the wars the line was used for a couple of interesting experiments with diesel railcars. In 1935 a pneumatic-tyred French-built railcar was tried out, while three years later a three-coach lightweight articulated train operated an experimental express service along the line. World War 2 again brought increased traffic, and in order to provide alternative routes for vital freight traffic in the event of air raid damage, a double track spur was laid in from Girtford to the GN line north of Sandy in September 1940. A passenger halt had been opened on 1 January 1938 at Girtford, where passengers could purchase tickets at a nearby garage, but closed on 17 November 1940, although the vegetable siding survived until 1 November 1951. Traffic over the line became even greater when an oil storage depot was opened on Sandy Heath in 1943, but after the war the Bedford-Cambridge line returned to its humdrum but useful existence, and in due course the connection to the GN main line was lifted after a period of use for wagon storage.

In later years the fortunes of the line fluctuated rapidly. In the mid-1950s concern was expressed about the congestion caused by the transfer of freight traffic across London, and in a project designed to utilise more fully cross-country lines outside London, the whole of the Oxford-Cambridge line was scheduled for development as the main northern artery. A reversing loop was planned at Sandy to enable GN line trains to gain access, and it was estimated that at least 30 trains each day would use the route. In the event, the plan was shelved and only the flyover at Bletchley remains as a reminder of the scheme.

In May 1959, British Railways announced proposals for the closure of many stations and lines. The Oxford-Cambridge line was among them – rather surprisingly, as it was difficult to believe that there was no market potential even for a limited-stop diesel service with suitable connections at each of the main lines which it crossed. Perhaps the projected increase in freight traffic had some influence on the proposals, but nevertheless the resultant public outcry caused the decision to be reversed, and a reprieve came within a few weeks. Diesel multiple-units were introduced on most services from 2 November of the same year, although the threat of closure still remained, with a further review projected two years later.

The Beeching Report of 1962 only proposed closure of intermediate stations, as it was felt that population growth in the main centres would ensure its future. Nevertheless, in December 1963 complete closure was once again proposed, when BR revealed a revenue of only £102,200 against expenditure of £199,700. Despite the usual difficulties with replacement buses, and an ultimately successful battle to keep the line open between Bletchley and Bedford, the target closing date for the line between Bedford and Cambridge was set for 3 January 1966. Through freight traffic ceased from 18 April 1966 (facilities having been withdrawn from Sandy on 4 February 1963 and from Potton on 1 January 1966), but passenger services survived for another two years. Complete closure between Goldington Ground Frame, on the outskirts of Bedford, and Cambridge Goods Yard took place from 1 January 1968.

A proposal to form a preservation society for the line between Sandy and Potton found favour locally, but those involved were unable to raise the purchase money, and track lifting started in July 1969. Thus the possibility, albeit remote, that *Shannon* could return to its original home was lost for ever. At Sandy the B&C buildings have vanished with a remodelling of the station, and the construction of a new road bridge in 1977, but at Potton they still remain in a fine state of preservation, complete with station signs and canopy. At Potton, too, the S&P engine shed is now in use as a market gardener's store – a less prestigious relic than *Shannon*, no doubt, but still a visible reminder of Captain Peel and his railway.

Below :
Photographed on 20 February 1982, the former B & C station at Potton is maintained in a fine state of preservation by its railway enthusiast owner.
J. M. Tolson

Bottom:
Although closed in 1862, the old Sandy & Potton engine shed at Potton still survives as a market gardener's store in a vegetable field. *J. M. Tolson*

Tailpiece
Steam on the South Devon Main Line

1985 was the year of GW150 and the return of steam to the Bristol–Plymouth main line. After the difficulties of the outwad run the previous day, No. 4930 *Hagley Hall* **and No. 7819** *Hinton Manor* **(both from the Severn Valley Railway) make a fine sight wih the return Plymouth–Bristol 'Great Western Limited' at Ivybridge on Easter Monday 8 April 1985.**
Brian Dobbs